Language Teaching:
A Scheme for Teacher Education

Editors: C N Candlin and H G Widdowson

Speaking

Martin Bygate

Oxford University Press

Oxford University Press
Great Clarendon Street, Oxford OX2 6DP

Oxford New York
Athens Auckland Bangkok Bogotá Buenos Aires
Calcutta Cape Town Chennai Dar es Salaam Delhi
Florence Hong Kong Istanbul Karachi Kuala Lumpur
Madrid Melbourne Mexico City Mumbai Nairobi Paris
São Paulo Shanghai Singapore Taipei Tokyo Toronto Warsaw

and associated companies in
Berlin Ibadan

OXFORD and OXFORD ENGLISH are trade marks of
Oxford University Press

ISBN 0 19 437134 4

© Oxford University Press 1987

First published 1987
Eighth impression 2000

Typeset in Bristol by Wyvern Typesetting Ltd.
Printed in Hong Kong

Acknowledgements

The publisher would like to thank the following for their
permission to reproduce material that falls within their copyright:
The author for three extracts from *Conversational Style:
Analyzing Talk Among Friends* (1984) by Deborah Tannen.
Cambridge University Press for five dialogues and a figure from *Communicative
Language Teaching* (1981) by William Littlewood.
Longman UK Ltd for ten activities from *Challenges* (1978) by Brian Abbs *et al.*
and for an exercise from *Progressive Picture Composition* (1967) by Donn Byrne.
Methuen and Co. Ltd. for five extracts from *The Birthday Party* (1960, revised
1965) by Harold Pinter.
NFER/Nelson Publishing Company Ltd. for a figure from *Simulations* (1979)
by D. Herbert and G. Sturtridge.
Unwin Hyman for an exercise from *Tandem* (published in 1981 by Evans
Brothers) by Alan Matthews and Carol Read.

Contents

Section Two: The methodology of oral interaction

The author and series editors

Martin Bygate is a graduate of the University of Leicester, where he read French. He holds an MA in Linguistics from the University of Manchester and a Ph.D from the University of London Institute of Education. He has worked as a teacher-trainer in a number of countries including France, Morocco, Brazil, Spain, and Italy, and at the University of Reading, and currently lectures at the School of Education, University of Leeds. His professional interests include second language acquisition, oral second language development, and tasks for language learning and teaching. He is also Co-editor of *Applied Linguistics* Journal.

Christopher N. Candlin is Chair Professor of Applied Linguistics and Director of the centre for English Language Education and Communication Research at the City University of Hong Kong. His previous post was as Professor of Linguistics in the School of English, Linguistics, and Media, and Executive Director of the National Centre for English Language Teaching and Research at Macquarie University, Sydney, having earlier been Professor of Applied Linguistics and Director of the Centre for Language in Social Life at the University of Lancaster. He also co-founded and directed the Institute for English Language Education at Lancaster, where he focused on issues in in-service education for teachers and teacher professional development.

Henry Widdowson, previously Professor of English for Speakers of Other Languages at the University of London Institute of Education, and Professor of Applied Linguistics at the University of Essex, is Professor of English Linguistics at the University of Vienna. He was previously Lecturer in Applied Linguistics at the University of Edinburgh, and has also worked as an English Language Officer for The British Council in Sri Lanka and Bangladesh.

Through work with The British Council, The Council of Europe, and other agencies, both Editors have had extensive and varied experience of language teaching, teacher education, and curriculum development overseas, and both contribute to seminars, conferences, and professional journals.

Introduction

Speaking

Development in language teaching must depend partly on our ability to understand the effects of our methodology. Usually responsibility for evaluating language-learning tasks is left to the specialist researchers, materials writers, and methodologists. However, an alternative view would be that – given the difficulties in obtaining, generalizing, and communicating research results, as well as the fact that in any case sophisticated teaching depends very largely on teachers' self-critical awareness – the results of specialist research can have only limited relevance: the most important single factor is the teachers' own understanding of the effects of their decisions. It is therefore worth focusing on the classroom effects of language-learning tasks. This is the approach adopted in this book.

Of course it is not possible to understand all the consequences of everything that we as teachers do in the classroom. However, of our repertoire of exercises and activities, some occur sufficiently often for it to be worth exploring their effects. The particular exercises of interest here are those devoted to developing speaking.

Speaking is in many ways an undervalued skill. Perhaps this is because we can almost all speak, and so take the skill too much for granted. Speaking is often thought of as a 'popular' form of expression which uses the unprestigious 'colloquial' register: literary skills are on the whole more prized. This relative neglect may perhaps also be due to the fact that speaking is transient and improvised, and can therefore be viewed as facile, superficial, or glib. And could it be that the negative aspects of behaviourist teaching techniques – which focused largely on the teaching of oral language – have become associated with the skill itself?

Speaking is, however, a skill which deserves attention every bit as much as literary skills, in both first and second languages. Our learners often need to be able to speak with confidence in order to carry out many of their most basic transactions. It is the skill by which they are most frequently judged, and through which they may make or lose friends. It is the vehicle *par excellence* of social solidarity, of social ranking, of professional advancement and of business. It is also a medium through which much language is learnt, and which for many is particularly conducive for learning. Perhaps, then, the teaching of speaking merits more thought.

The aim of this book is to outline some ways in which we may be able to get a better understanding of how our learners learn to speak a foreign language through the various tasks which can be made available to them. The book is in three parts. In the first part we consider some of the things that are involved in the apparently simple task of speaking to someone. In the second part we review some of the principal types of activities and exercises used to teach speaking. In the final part of the book we outline ways in which the teacher can explore what learners do and what they learn through oral classroom activities. In each part of the book the reader-teacher is invited to check the argument by means of small activities or by observing what his or her learners do in various tasks.

Many people have contributed directly or indirectly to the writing of this book. They include notably the English staff and students of the Languages Department at the Federal University of Santa Catarina, Brazil; Peter Hill and Peter Skehan at the University of London Institute of Education; Cristina Whitecross and Simon Murison-Bowie of Oxford University Press; Chris Candlin and Henry Widdowson, who have of course left a deep influence on the substance and shape of the book; and last but most enduringly my wife Anne. To all I express my appreciation; and my apologies for any inadequacies.

Martin Bygate

Language Teaching:
A Scheme for Teacher Education

The purpose of this scheme of books is to engage language teachers in a process of continual professional development. We have designed it so as to guide teachers towards the critical appraisal of ideas and the informed application of these ideas in their own classrooms. The scheme provides the means for teachers to take the initiative themselves in pedagogic planning. The emphasis is on critical enquiry as a basis for effective action.

We believe that advances in language teaching stem from the independent efforts of teachers in their own classrooms. This independence is not brought about by imposing fixed ideas and promoting fashionable formulas. It can only occur where teachers, individually or collectively, explore principles and experiment with techniques. Our purpose is to offer guidance on how this might be achieved.

The scheme consists of three sub-series of books covering areas of enquiry and practice of immediate relevance to language teaching and learning. Sub-series 1 focuses on areas of *language knowledge*, with books linked to the conventional levels of linguistic description: pronunciation, vocabulary, grammar, and discourse. Sub-series 2 (of which this present volume forms a part) focuses on different *modes of behaviour* which realize this knowledge. It is concerned with the pedagogic skills of speaking, listening, reading, and writing. Sub-series 3 focuses on a variety of *modes of action* which are needed if this knowledge and behaviour is to be acquired in the operation of language teaching. The books in this sub-series have do with such topics as syllabus design, the content of language courses, and aspects of methodology and evaluation.

This sub-division of the field is not meant to suggest that different topics can be dealt with in isolation. On the contrary, the concept of a scheme implies making coherent links between all these different areas of enquiry and activity. We wish to emphasize how their integration formalizes the complex factors present in any teaching process. Each book, then, highlights a particular topic, but also deals contingently with other issues, themselves treated as focal in other books in the series. Clearly, an enquiry into a mode of behaviour like speaking, for example, must also refer to aspects of language knowledge which it realizes. It must also connect to modes of action which can be directed at developing this behaviour in learners. As elements of the whole scheme, therefore, books cross-refer both within and across the different sub-series.

This principle of cross-reference which links the elements of the scheme is also applied to the internal design of the different inter-related books within it. Thus, each book contains three sections, which, by a combination of text and task, engage the reader in a principled enquiry into ideas and practices. The first section of each book makes explicit those theoretical ideas which bear on the topic in question. It provides a conceptual framework for those sections which follow. Here the text has a mainly *explanatory* function, and the tasks serve to clarify and consolidate the points raised. The second section shifts the focus of attention to how the ideas from Section One relate to activities in the classroom. Here the text is concerned with *demonstration*, and the tasks are designed to get readers to evaluate suggestions for teaching in reference both to the ideas from Section One and also to their own teaching experience. In the third section this experience is projected into future work. Here the set of tasks, modelled on those in Section Two, are designed to be carried out by the reader as a combination of teaching techniques and action research in the actual classroom. It is this section that renews the reader's contact with reality: the ideas expounded in Section One and linked to pedagogic practice in Section Two are now to be systematically *tested out* in the process of classroom teaching.

If language teaching is to be a genuinely professional enterprise, it requires continual experimentation and evaluation on the part of practitioners whereby in seeking to be more effective in their pedagogy they provide at the same time—and as a corollary—for their own continuing education. It is our aim in this scheme to promote this dual purpose.

Christopher N. Candlin
Henry Widdowson

Understanding speaking

1 Speaking as a skill

1.1 Knowledge and skill

One of the basic problems in foreign-language teaching is to prepare learners to be able to use the language. How this preparation is done, and how successful it is, depends very much on how we as teachers understand our aims. For instance, it is obvious that in order to be able to speak a foreign language, it is necessary to know a certain amount of grammar and vocabulary. Part of a language course is therefore generally devoted to this objective. But there are other things involved in speaking, and it is important to know what these might be, so that they too can be included in our teaching.

For instance, to test whether learners can speak, it is necessary to get them to actually say something. To do this they must act on a knowledge of grammar and vocabulary. By giving learners 'speaking practice' and 'oral exams' we recognize that there is a difference between *knowledge* about a language, and *skill* in using it. This distinction between knowledge and skill is crucial in the teaching of speaking.

An analogy with the driver of a car may be helpful. What knowledge does a car driver need? Clearly he or she needs to *know* the names of the controls; where they are; what they do and how they are operated (you move the pedals with your feet, not with your hands). However, the driver also needs the *skill* to be able to use the controls to guide the car along a road without hitting the various objects that tend to get in the way; you have to be able to do this at a normal speed (you can fail your driving test in Britain for driving too slowly or hesitantly); you have to drive smoothly and without getting too close to any dangerous obstacles. And it is not enough to drive in a straight line: the driver also has to be able to manage the variations in road conditions safely.

In a way, the job we do when we speak is similar. We do not merely *know* how to assemble sentences in the abstract: we have to produce them and adapt them to the circumstances. This means making decisions rapidly, implementing them smoothly, and adjusting our conversation as unexpected problems appear in our path.

▶ ## TASK 1

Knowledge itself is not enough: knowledge has to be used in action. This is true not only of using language but of any other activity. Here are some examples. Are the statements true or false?

T 1 It is possible to know the rules of football but not be much good at playing.

T 2 It is possible to be a good cook but not know many recipes.

F 3 If you explain to someone just how to ride a bicycle, then they ought to be able to get straight on to one and ride away.

T 4 You can be sure that if a learner omits the third person -s on the verb it is because he or she does not know it.

F 5 All you need to be a good teacher is to know your subject well.

Can you find any evidence—from your experience or from common knowledge—which will help you decide whether these statements are true or false? Can you think of two other examples of activities where knowledge is not enough for successful performance?

If we think about how we use our first language, then it is obvious that we spend most of our time using sentences, and very little of our time reviewing our knowledge or trying to compose perfect sentences. We would find it most difficult to describe and explain all the decisions we take when we speak. So knowledge is only a part of the affair: we also need skill.

What is the difference between knowledge and skill? A fundamental difference is that while both can be understood and memorized, only a skill can be imitated and practised.

▶ ## TASK 2

This can be illustrated. There are various ways of helping a learner: explanation, memorization, demonstration, and practice.

1 Which tactic would you use if you thought that the learner:
   a. had not understood a point; *Expl. + demo, practise*
   b. had completely forgotten something; *memo, expl pract.*
   c. did not know of the existence of a rule or word; *explan, memo, pract*
   d. was not used to doing the activity; *practise*
   e. panicked? *expl, practise*

2 Below is a list of difficulties a learner might encounter in a variety of activities. In each case decide what sort of remedies would be useful:

   a. When changing gear, a friend learning to drive a car produces a horrible grating sound. *pract*
   b. A child is learning to break an egg, but smashes the shell into little bits, losing half the egg on the table and missing the bowl. *pract*

    c. Your friend says she is no good at jigsaw puzzles. *pract*

    d. You are trying to help someone learn to read. *exp, pract*

    e. Someone says that he is no good at remembering names at parties, and that it is getting embarrassing. *memo, pract*

In any of the above situations, did you find that practice was irrelevant?

So one of the main reasons for clarifying the distinction between knowledge and skill is that problems in each area may require different pedagogical actions. We will now look more closely at what we mean by 'skill'.

1.2 Oral skills and interaction

There are two basic ways in which something we do can be seen as a skill. First there are motor-perceptive skills. But in addition to this there are also interaction skills. Let us see the difference between the two. First the motor-perceptive skills.

Motor-perceptive skills involve perceiving, recalling, and articulating in the correct order sounds and structures of the language. This is the relatively superficial aspect of skill which is a bit like learning how to manipulate the controls of a car on a deserted piece of road far from the flow of normal traffic. It is the context-free kind of skill, the kind which has been recognized in language teaching for many years in the rationale of the audio-lingual approach to language teaching. For example, twenty years ago, W. F. Mackey summarized oral expression as follows:

> Oral expression involves not only [. . .] the use of the right sounds in the right patterns of rhythm and intonation, but also the choice of words and inflections in the right order to convey the right meaning.
> (1965: 266)

Notice how much importance Mackey gives to doing things 'right' in order to be any good at speaking: choosing the right forms; putting them in the correct order; sounding like a native speaker; even producing the right meanings. (Is this how people learn to handle the clutch and gear lever?)

This view of language skill influences the list of exercises which Mackey discusses: model dialogues, pattern practice, oral drill tables, look-and-say exercises, and oral composition. However, this is a bit like learning to drive without ever going out on the road.

Ten years later, during which time this approach to teaching oral skills had been widely adopted, David Wilkins pointed out there were some learning problems that exercises like these did not solve. An important one is that of ensuring a satisfactory transition from supervised learning in the classroom to real-life use of the skill. This transition is often called the 'transfer of skills'. As Wilkins points out, if *all* language produced in the classroom is determined by the teacher, 'we are protecting [the learner] from the additional burden of having to make his own choices'. He continues:

> As with everything else he will only learn what falls within his experience. If all his language production is controlled from outside, he will hardly be competent to control his own language production. *He will not be able to transfer his knowledge from a language-learning situation to a language-using situation.*
> (1975:76, my italics)

Nor, presumably, will the learner be able to transfer much of any motor-perceptive skill to a 'language-using situation'. The point is that in addition to the motor-perceptive skills there are other skills to be developed, which, as Wilkins says, are those of 'controlling one's own language production' and 'having to make one's own choices'. This kind of skill we will call *interaction skill*. This is the skill of using knowledge and basic motor-perception skills to achieve communication. Let us look at what interaction skills basically involve.

Interaction skills involve making decisions about communication, such as: what to say, how to say it, and whether to develop it, in accordance with one's intentions, while maintaining the desired relations with others. Note that our notions of what is right or wrong now depend on such things as what we have decided to say, how successful we have been so far, whether it is useful to continue the point, what our intentions are, and what sorts of relations we intend to establish or maintain with our interlocutors. This of course is true of all communication, in speech or in writing.

▶ ## TASK 3

Here is a list of things that we tend to teach and test in language courses. Which are only examples of *motor-perceptive skills* and which are also examples of *interaction skills*?

1 Show an ability to produce at least 35 of the 40 phonemes in British English. *m*

2 Form the perfect tense correctly with *have* followed by the past participle of the lexical verb. *m*

3 Be able to ask someone the time. *i*

4 Have the ability to introduce yourself to someone you have never met. *i*

5 Be able to use *at* correctly with expressions of time and place. *m*

6 Show an ability to describe your flat or home clearly to a decorator or estate agent. *i*

7 Be able to use correctly the three finite forms of lexical verbs. *m*

8 Be able to use the telephone to obtain information about train/plane/bus times.

If you were to test these language abilities, which would be easiest to test by asking for one correct answer?

Interaction skills involve the ability to use language in order to satisfy particular demands. There are at least two demands which can affect the nature of speech. The first of these is related to the internal conditions of speech: the fact that speech takes place under the pressure of time. These we shall call *processing conditions*. A second kind involves the dimension of interpersonal interaction in conversation. These we might call *reciprocity conditions*. First, what are the main effects of the processing conditions on speech?

It generally makes a difference whether a piece of communication is carefully prepared or whether it is composed on the spur of the moment. This can affect our choice of words and our style. Similar effects can be observed of the restrictions of time or money when imposed on film-makers, painters, composers, architects, and builders. The scale of the output may be affected. So too might the materials, and the internal structure.

▶ **TASK 4**

Time constraints affect performance. To see how this might be relevant to language teaching, consider once again teaching someone to drive. Suppose that on a deserted track your learner's physical handling of the car is perfect. That is, he or she can start, stop, change gear, steer, and use all the other controls and indicators perfectly well. However, your impression is that it is all far too slow. What pressures should the learner be prepared for? How can a learner be prepared before going out on to the public roads?

In spoken interaction the time constraint can be expected to have observable effects. Brown and Yule, for instance, suggest that it is possible to distinguish between 'short speaking turns' and 'long speaking turns' (1983: 27ff). 'Long turns' tend to be more prepared—like an after-dinner speech or a talk on the radio.

'Short turns' are the more common. In this case the wording and the subject matter tend to be worked out extempore as the speaking proceeds. The differences in form undoubtedly reflect the differences in decision-making on the part of the speaker. Some of these differences, as Brown and Yule point out, include the fact that 'native speakers typically produce bursts of speech which are much more readily relateable to the phrase—typically shorter than sentences, and only loosely strung together'. Very different from written language. And they add:

> If native speakers typically produce short, phrase-sized chunks, it
> seems perverse to demand that foreign learners should be expected
> to produce complete sentences. Indeed it may demand of them, in
> the foreign language, a capacity for forward-planning and storage
> which they rarely manifest in speaking their own native language.
> (1983:26)

Processing conditions are an important influence. The ability to master the
processing conditions of speech enables speakers to deal fluently with a
given topic while being listened to. This kind of ability thus covers the basic
communicative skill of producing speech at a normal speed under pressure
of time. This is generally not a problem in first-language learning, but it can
be with learners who have used the language only in written form, or with
heavy emphasis on accuracy.

▶ **TASK 5**

Consider how far the following activities help to prepare learners for
this dimension of language use:

1 reading aloud;
2 giving a prepared talk;
3 learning a long piece of text or dialogue by heart;
4 interviewing someone, or being interviewed;
5 doing a drill.

Of course, time pressure is not the only constraint that causes problems to
speakers. We have already mentioned that speakers do not work from
prepared scripts. What they decide to say is affected by the second
condition of speech, the *reciprocity condition*.

The reciprocity condition of speech refers to the relation between the
speaker and listener in the process of speech (see for instance Widdowson
1978, Chapter 6). The term 'reciprocity' enables us to distinguish between
those situations in which both the speaker and hearer are allowed to speak,
and those where conventionally, only the speaker has speaking rights, as
during a speech. The reciprocal dimension affects speech because there is
more than one participant. The business of making sure that the
conversation works is shared by both participants: there are at least two
addressees and two decision-makers.

For example, in a reciprocal exchange, a speaker will often have to adjust
his or her vocabulary and message to take the listener into account. The
speaker also has to participate actively in the interlocutor's message—
asking questions, reacting, and so on. This is something which requires an
ability to be flexible in communication, and a learner may need to be
prepared for it.

▶ TASK 6

Reciprocity conditions affect skills in the first, second, or any language. Let us take a simple topic, for example, talking about yourself. Does it make any difference who of the following people you are speaking to? Are some situations usually easier than others? In what ways?

1 At an interview for a job.
2 At a dinner given in your honour by your colleagues.
3 To a close friend.
4 Directly to a television camera.
5 With your eyes closed.
6 To four friends.
7 To four strangers.
8 Into a tape recorder.
9 To a class of thirty.

In the following well-known extract from *Much Ado About Nothing*, how far are Dogberry's mistakes a problem of lack of processing skills, how far a matter of interaction skill?

> **Don Pedro**: Officers, what offence hath these men done?
> **Dogberry**: Marry, sir, they have committed false report; moreover they have spoken untruths; secondarily, they are slanders; sixth and lastly, they have belied a lady; thirdly, they have verified unjust things; and, to conclude, they are lying knaves.
> (Act V, Scene i)

The main topic of this book, then, is to discuss ways in which speakers effectively use knowledge for reciprocal interaction under normal processing conditions, and to explore ways in which the ability to do this can be developed in foreign-language or second-language learners. We have seen that knowledge and skill are distinct aspects of foreign-language ability, and that skill itself can be seen to be of two kinds, motor-perceptive skill and interaction skill. Let us now look at how the skills of reciprocal oral interaction differ from those of written interaction.

knowledge   skill

motor-perceptive   interaction skill

2   Differences between speech and writing

2.1 Introduction

Speech is not spoken writing. White (1978) comments that we tend to be
critical about people who 'speak like a book'. This is partly because books
are not generally addressed to individual people, or written in the way that
people talk, and so the style of written language may often sound odd when
spoken. The vocabulary may be formal or elaborate, the sentences long and
complex. It may also seem as though the speaker was not in fact speaking to
you, but to a public gathering.

▶ TASK 7

One feature of books is that the reader can skim, scan, jump
forwards and backwards, and omit sections he or she already knows
about. It does not matter too much if books include information
which a particular reader already knows. How does this compare
with the normal position of someone listening to a speaker?

Of course if you have actually tried to 'speak like a book' yourself, you may
agree that it can be hard work. It is hard work *reading* aloud from a book.
This may be because it is not something we are used to; or because the
sentences can be awkward to read aloud—too long, too complex, or too
technical. It can be tricky to get the correct intonation, and you may find
you often have to re-read bits to make them sound right. Reading aloud
tends to require considerable attention.

▶ TASK 8

Try reading aloud, either in your own or in a foreign language. Tape
your first attempt, including any mistakes. Then consider the
following questions:

How did it feel: easy, tiring, enjoyable? Try to explain your answer.
Were you aware of any mistakes? On listening to your recording, did
you find any other mistakes? What were they, and why do you think
they occurred? Do you think your reading was as intelligible as
possible?

So speaking like a book is, in two words, disagreeable and difficult. This is because written language is ill-adjusted to the two sets of conditions mentioned previously, namely the processing conditions, and the conditions of reciprocity. Let us look at these two factors.

2.2 Processing conditions of speech and writing

The main features of speaking which can be traced to the processing conditions of communication involve the time factor. The words are being spoken as they are being decided and as they are being understood.

The fact that they are being spoken *as they are being decided* affects the speaker's ability to plan and organize the message, and to control the language being used. The speaker's sentences cannot be as long or as complex as in writing, because the writer has more time to plan. In speech we often make syntactic mistakes because we lose our place in the grammar of our utterances. Mistakes are also made in both the message and the wording; we forget things we intended to say; the message is not so economically organized as it might be in print; we may even forget what we have already said, and repeat ourselves.

The words are also being spoken *as they are being understood.* Once spoken, they are gone. While the reader can reread, the listener can have memory problems which can lead to misunderstandings, or to a request for a repetition. Furthermore, the listener may miss a part of what was said, perhaps through noise, or a moment's distraction. All these are very good reasons for not speaking like a book.

 TASK 9

Of the following two stretches of discourse by a native speaker, one was spoken, the other edited. Which do you think was originally spoken? What indications are there?

1 speaking impressionistically it would appear that if a word is fairly high on the frequency list the chances are you would get a compound or another phonologically deviant form frequently of the same phonological shape –

2 and it seems to be if a word is fairly high on the frequency list I have not made any count but just impressionistically um um the chances are that you get a compound or another phonologically deviant form with ah which is already in other words which is fairly frequently the same phonological shape –
(after Pawley and Syder, 1983)

The form of spoken language, then, is affected by the time limitations, and the associated problems of planning, memory, and of production under pressure. Things may not always go according to the ideal plan. At the same time, the resulting conventions of spoken language are different in certain important respects from those of written language. We will see how that might be in a moment. First let us look at the second main difference between speech and writing.

2.3 Reciprocity conditions of speech and writing

The second feature of speech which is of considerable importance is that it is a reciprocal activity. This crucially affects the sorts of decisions that are likely to be made.

In most speaking, the person we are speaking to is in front of us and able to put us right if we make a mistake. He or she can also generally show agreement and understanding—or incomprehension and disagreement. This makes a big difference from most types of writing, and it compensates in large part for the limitations that derive from the processing conditions.

In written communication a considerable part of the skill comes from both the reader's and the writer's ability to imagine the other's point of view. A writer has to anticipate the reader's understanding and predict potential problems. In doing this the writer has to make guesses about what the reader knows and does not know, about what the reader will be able to understand, and even about what the reader will want to read. If the writer gets this wrong, the reader may give up the book or article in disgust before getting far.

Readers, of course, are in a similar position, because if something is not clear to them, or if it is already so clear that they do not need to read it, then they have no way of signalling this to the writer. Readers therefore have to put in some compensatory work in order to make their reading successful: either skip, or else work very carefully. Both readers and writers need patience and imagination at a communicative level.

Speakers on the other hand, are in a different position. They may need patience and imagination too, but to make sure that communication is taking place, they have to pay attention to their listeners and adapt their messages according to their listeners' reaction. With the help of these reactions, the message can be adjusted from moment to moment, understanding can be improved, and the speaker's task is therefore facilitated.

▶ TASK 10

Consider the following dialogue. Are the speakers incompetent? How do they exploit the presence of the interlocutor?

Teacher: Morning, Mrs Williams. I've brought the money.
Secretary: Oh, hello Mr James. What money?
Teacher: You know, the money for the books.

Secretary: The money for what books?
Teacher: Oh, I thought that Mrs Prior had told you about the reading books for the third years.
Secretary: Oh yes, they've been ordered.
Teacher: So where shall I put it?
Secretary: What? . . . oh over there on the filing cabinet . . .

How might Mr James have communicated in writing?

However, more than this, speakers in fact *must* take notice of such feedback, because if they do not, they will be seen as socially obtuse, perhaps distant or arrogant, and maybe stupid: if someone is signalling to you that they have perfectly understood something, or already know about it, it would look odd if you ploughed on with a prepared speech.

▶ **TASK 11**

Look again at the preceding dialogue. Explain why the communication could not have started in the same way if it had been conducted in writing.

Reciprocity may be an advantage, compensating for the irregularities and messiness of speech. But it is also an obligation. It forces us to take notice of the other, and to allow him or her also the chance to speak. We take turns at speaking: it forces us and enables us to adjust to what the other person knows; it forces us to take notice of new mutual knowledge during conversation; it involves varying our degree of formality according to the individual we are speaking to; and it enables us or obliges us to choose or develop topics of conversation which are likely to be of some interest to the other party.

If the processing conditions act as a limitation on our capacity for expression, affecting perhaps the size of the units we use, reciprocity is the condition which challenges us to show continual sensitivity and an ability to adjust our use of the language. These are the conditions which help to characterize the use of spoken language. They affect the way the forms of language are utilized. We will look at this more closely in the following unit.

3   Production skills

3.1 Introduction

The way language is organized in speech is typically different from the shape it takes in writing. The language may be the same one (recognizably English, Russian or Spanish, for instance), but the size and shape of its sentences tends to be different. This should not surprise us. After all, we take it for granted that pop music, jazz, and orchestral music use the same notes and scales but differ in the way these resources are put together. The same can be said of spoken and written language. And the reason for this is largely to do with the time constraints under which the language is produced.

We are calling these constraints 'processing conditions', and they affect the speaker: in order to get his message out, he is likely to arrange language and communicate meanings in a different way from if he were writing. Sometimes this helps him to produce his message and get it right, and sometimes it also helps the listener.

As we have already seen, one of the most important of the constraints is time pressure: oral language allows limited time for deciding what to say, deciding how to say it, saying it, and checking that the speaker's main intentions are being realized.

Time pressure tends to affect the language used in at least two main ways. Firstly, speakers use devices in order to *facilitate* production, and secondly they often have to *compensate* for the difficulties.

Because speakers have less time to plan, organize and execute their message, they are often exploring their phrasing and their meaning as they speak. This gives rise to four common features of spoken language. Firstly, it is easier for speakers to improvise if they use less complex syntax. In addition, because of time pressure, people take short cuts to avoid unnecessary effort in producing individual utterances. This often leads speakers to abbreviate the message and produce 'incomplete' sentences or clauses, omitting unnecessary elements where possible. This is known as 'ellipsis'. Thirdly, it is easier for speakers to produce their message if they use fixed conventional phrases. And finally, it is inevitable that they will use devices to gain time to speak. All of these devices facilitate production.

▶ TASK 12

How do teachers usually treat ellipsis when it occurs in the speech of learners?

How might students' use of simplification and ellipsis help or hinder (a) the learning of structures and (b) oral practice?

In considering compensation, we are concerned with the way speakers find themselves repeating, in various ways, what they have already said. The fact that speakers find themselves 'feeling out what they are going to say' as they say it induces various kinds of errors. As a result, it is quite common for speakers to find themselves correcting or improving what they have already said. In a sense what they are doing is *compensating* for the problems which arise out of the time pressure. What's more, time pressure also increases pressure on *memory*: in order to ensure clear understanding, speakers therefore use a lot of repetitions and rephrasings.

▶ TASK 13

Consider once again the problems of oral accuracy. How important is it for foreign-language speakers to speak without errors or hesitations?

Given these features, how, in general terms, might we approach the problem of evaluating learners' oral production?

In the remainder of this unit we will first consider what language use these features imply. We will then study some reasons why these phenomena can be important for both speaker and listener, particularly when the speaker or listener is a learner.

3.2 Facilitation

There are four main ways in which speakers can facilitate production of speech:

by simplifying structure;
by ellipsis;
by using formulaic expressions;
by the use of fillers and hesitation devices.

The first feature, simplification, largely involves *parataxis*. Let us look at what this is.

Simplification can be found mainly in the tendency to tack new sentences on to previous ones by the use of coordinating conjunctions like 'and', 'or', 'but', or indeed no conjunction at all. This way of connecting sentences is called 'parataxis'. Instead of parataxis, a speaker might use 'hypotaxis', that is, subordination. Subordination, however, often involves more complex sentence-planning. While in writing we have time to use a lot of subordination, time pressures in speech often tend to make the use of subordination more difficult. So parataxis can be understood as a simplification strategy in the production of speech.

In addition to parataxis, speakers often avoid complex noun groups with many adjectives preceding them. Instead, they tend to repeat the same sentence structure to add further adjectives separately. As a result, oral language tends to be more 'spread out' and less dense than written language.

► TASK 14

In the following passage a non-native speaker is describing a picture. Note any of the features discussed above under parataxis and the avoidance of complex noun groups:

> OK—in this picture in picture—er—number 1 I can see er a little girl—who probably—is inside—her house—er who is playing—with a bear—this bear—it has a brown colour—and—the little girl is sitting—in the—in the stairs of her house—this house is very nice—it has rugs—it has—brown rugs—mm—it has waste basket

Ellipsis is also used to facilitate production when time is short. This consists of the omission of parts of a sentence, like syntactic abbreviation. Examples include: 'Who?', 'On Saturday', 'the big one', 'does what', 'Why me?' 'Green'. In order to understand, a listener must have a good idea of the background knowledge assumed by the speaker. In most speech situations this can be counted on. Thus for example, when someone says 'Look', 'Why don't you come out?', or 'John knows', the speaker and listener both know (although a hearer might not), what there is to look at, what the person could come out of, and what John knows. In order to speak economically, it is necessary and normal to exploit ellipsis: we do not always speak in complete sentences.

► TASK 15

Short cuts can often help speakers to get to the point, although they can give rise to ambiguities for people who have not been following the conversation or do not know the context. In what ways are the speakers being economical in the following utterances?

1 F: I wonder where they'd get their food from?
   P: Kill them.
   F: Ah yes.

2 **M**: in the old—or in the young continents
   T: erm the young continents—the young continent
   M: in the young continent—America
   T: mhm
   M: it's in America—South America
   T: South America
   M: near Peru
   T: near

Compare the previous extracts with the following.

3 Answer in complete sentences.

What is your name? . . . My name is John.
Where do you live? . . . I live in Canterbury.
What is your address? . . . My address is 19 The Green.

Did you enjoy the cinema the other day? . . . No, I didn't enjoy the cinema the other day. The cinema the other day was closed.

Do such answers need to be in full sentences?

A third tool used for facilitating the production of spoken language consists of sets of conventional 'colloquial' or idiomatic expressions or phrases. These are sometimes called *formulaic expressions*. They consist of all kinds of set expressions, not just idioms, but also phrases which have more normal meanings, but which just tend to go together. Michael Stubbs gives the following examples:

1 (In a bar) Have this one on me.
2 I don't believe a word of it.
3 Who does he think he is?
4 I thought you'd never ask.
5 It's very nice to meet you.
(Stubbs 1983:155)

Pawley and Syder (1983:206–7) give many more. Although all the words in these phrases have their normal meanings, some of them are difficult to change (try 'I don't believe a sentence of it', or 'Who does he believe he is?', or 'It's very agreeable to meet you').

Our interest in these expressions is that they can contribute to oral fluency. Speakers do not have to monitor their choice of words one after another. They do not have to construct each new utterance afresh, using the rules of the grammar and their knowledge of vocabulary in order to vary their expression for each fresh occasion. Instead they proceed by using chunks which they have learnt as wholes. This is particularly important in routine situations.

► TASK 16

It can be difficult at first sight to pick out someone's use of formulaic expressions, since often you can only recognize them after listening to the speaker for a while. The following example may illustrate the way in which speakers put together what they have to say, using sequences of short learnt phrases (note: — = pause):

> OK—erm—a at the back [mhm] I mean er—in the office I also see a—this is a young lady [mhm] sitting in a chair [mhm] she might be a secretary [mhm] OK—it seems to me oh th this er little boy [mhm] this little boy seems to be—punished [mm] don't you see—he has er—he has his—his hands—in the back

Consider when you go into a bank. Think particularly of how you start to speak. Do you think that you carefully put together a brand-new set of sentences as you start? What evidence do you have for your opinion?

The final set of strategies used to facilitate the production of speech are *time-creating devices*. These tend to give speakers more time to formulate what they intend to say next. Features here include the use of fillers, pauses, and hesitations. One frequent kind of filler is the use of phrases like 'well', 'erm', 'you see', 'kind of', 'sort of', 'you know', and so on. Another kind of filler arises when speakers rephrase or repeat what they or their interlocutors have said. A final strategy is simply to hesitate, repeating words while trying to find a needed word. By doing this, they give themselves more time to find their words or organize their ideas.

3.3 Compensation

Because planning time is limited, speakers also often need to change what they have already said. In speech alterations are permitted—indeed they are quite common. In writing, of course, crossings out and alterations in the text should be kept to a minimum to facilitate reading. A reader may be confused or put off by a text full of corrections. Consequently the writer carefully rewrites sections so that they read clearly, as though no correction had been made.

In speech, however, corrections are tolerated and indeed necessary. What happens is that the speaker substitutes a noun or an adjective for another, or repeats a noun group, adjective or adverb with additional elements in order to alter some aspect of what he or she has said. This is a first reason for reformulation to occur.

TASK 17

In the following extracts, the speakers use certain strategies to give themselves time to plan, and they also use some simple self-correction features. Can you identify them?

> this picture and this picture I think I have er (. . .) in an airport or a place like that—erm—there are—oh six people—seven maybe—one is running out—the one of the rooms with a handbag—another one is—erm—drinking—coffee I think—probably (. . .) and there is a lady there is a lady passing by I suppose or observing—and a little boy and er what I suppose is—a kind of—window [yeah] in the corridor aand—ah no—there a six people but two of them are part of a—picture I think . . .

> mhm yeah all right yeah I I'm sure the picture I have comes er before the erm before the one er in the table erm in my picture I think er we should already start describing our pictures OK so we can say it quicker in my picture I see erm I see a fellow riding a bike [mhm] and er approaching to a corner [mhm] where we can see a truck it seems to me that th this fellow is not er looking is not looking at the truck which is er approaching the corner.

The second way in which time pressure affects oral language production is that the gist of the whole transaction has to be held in the speaker's memory. In order to make this easier, speakers tend to rephrase and reformulate what they say. This is often in order to give people time to understand, to remind them of things that were said.

These characteristics are all related to an important aspect of speech, which is that it is not recorded: it is only temporary. It is not possible for either speaker or listener to go back over previous speech if something was not understood. There are memory limitations. For this reason the organization of the structure of speech involves short bursts of language, back and forth between the speakers, so that people can comment freely on remarks made as they come up. Only in formal discussion is it often necessary to refer back to what someone said many minutes before. The features we have mentioned all help to reduce memory load, just as they help to lighten the planning load.

▶ TASK 18

Facilitating features include simplification; ellipsis; formulaic expressions; and fillers. Compensation features include self-correction; false starts; repetition; and rephrasing. Read the following passages and identify any of the features that occur. The first extract is taken from the recording of a native speaker describing an accident. (note:—= pause):

> 1 S: it's erm—an intersection of kind of two—a kind of crossroads—of a minor road going across a major road—and I was standing there—and there was this erm—kind of ordinary car—on the minor road—just looking to come out—onto the big road—and coming down towards him on the big road was a van—followed by a lorry—now—just as he started to come out onto the main road—the van—no the lorry star-started to overtake the van—not having seen the fact that another car was coming out
> (from Brown and Yule 1983:140)

> 2 G.D.: we had a fantastic time—there were all kinds of relations there I dunno where they all come from I didn't know 'alf o' them—and ah—the kids sat on the floor—and ol' Uncle Bert he ah o' course he was the life and soul of the party Uncle Bert 'ad a black bottle—an' ah–'e'd tell a few stories an' 'e'd take a sip out of the black bottle n' the more sips he took outa that bottle—the worse the stories got—
> (from Pawley and Syder, 1983:203)

So the processing conditions of oral language result in certain common language features. These are as follows:

adjustments: hesitations, false starts, self-corrections, rephrasings, and circumlocutions;
syntactic features: ellipsis and parataxis;
repetition: via expansion or reduction;
formulaic expressions.

3.4 Conclusion

Why might these features be important for learners and why should we as teachers be aware of them? Firstly, we can see how helpful it is for learners to be able to facilitate oral production by using these features, and how important it is for them to get used to compensating for the problems. Thus for instance in the classroom they may not need to produce full sentences every time they open their mouths. Parataxis too may be useful until learners develop a range of more complex ways of extending sentences. As they become more skilled in producing utterances, their use of these features may become more flexible. The use of formulaic expressions, hesitation devices, self-correction, rephrasing and repetition can also be expected to help learners become more fluent.

All these features may in fact *help* learners to speak, and hence help them to *learn* to speak. If we think of learners by definition as not being fluent in finding the words they need, or in structuring their utterances, then much of what we have been discussing is likely to be just as important in the foreign-language classroom as for native speakers. In addition to helping learners to learn to speak, these features may also help learners to sound *normal* in their use of the foreign language. This may be a further important consideration.

If these features occur naturally in learners' speech, this may affect us as teachers, because it may have implications for the way learners should work. It may also affect how we evaluate learners. If native and non-native speakers in normal interaction usually produce language with such characteristics, this may influence what we expect of our learners in oral activities and tests.

▶ ## TASK 19

Consider an athletics coach who has to train athletes, some of whom specialize in 100-metres races, and others in 3000-metres races. Do you think the coach would be justified in thinking that the skill of running varies according to the circumstances, and thus requires different training schedules? Is there an analogy with language learning?

In all, the production of speech in real time imposes pressures, but also allows freedoms which may enable learners to explore how a language can be made to work, at the same time as they improve their fluency in producing utterances. This, then, is the first aspect of speech, the production skills which are so important if anyone is to be able to interact with native speakers for real-life purposes. In the next section we consider some of the negotiating skills that speakers need to employ if their production skills are to be of any use.

4 Interaction skills

What you say to somebody depends not only on what he has said to you (though this is obviously very important) but also on what you want to get out of the conversation. The strategies and tactics involved in using language this way are of fundamental importance in communication. (Morrow 1981:63)

4.1 Introduction

In spoken interaction, speaker and listener do not merely have to be good processors of the spoken word, able to produce coherent language in the difficult circumstances of spoken communication. It is also useful if they are good communicators, that is, good at saying what they want to say in a way which the listener finds understandable. To appreciate what is involved, it can be useful to think of the communication of meaning as depending on two kinds of skill.

Firstly, in many circumstances speakers organize what they have to communicate in typical patterns. These patterns correspond more or less to typical kinds of message, and so deal with recurring cognitive problems. These have been called 'routines' (e.g. Widdowson 1983). Examples of routines include story telling or joke telling; descriptions or comparisons; and instructions.

Secondly speakers also develop skills in solving all sorts of communication problems which can be expected to occur in spoken exchanges. These we will call negotiation skills. They consist of skills which are used to enable speakers to make themselves clearly understood whatever the interaction, and to deal with communication problems that may occur. Negotiation skills are skills which are common to all kinds of communication. For example, they include the ability to check on specific meanings, to alter wording, to correct mistaken interpretations, to find words for ideas for which the speaker does not already have some generally accepted phrase.

We should perhaps note that these skills—they might almost be called thinking skills—are in many respects the same as those required in written communication, where they are equally important. However, both routines and negotiation skills are likely to involve slightly different forms of expression according to whether the language used is oral or written (for instance, a spoken story is likely to have some oral conventions which are less likely in written form).

4.2 Routines

Routines can be defined as 'conventional ways of presenting information'. Because they are conventional, they are predictable and help ensure clarity. There are two main kinds of routines: *information routines* and *interaction routines.*

Information routines

By 'information routines' we mean frequently recurring types of information structures, including stories; descriptions of places and people; presentation of facts; comparisons; instructions. As we have said, routines like these do not just concern speech; they also occur in written language. However, putting such information into speech is also likely to require practice under the conditions of normal speech.

▶ TASK 20

Statements like the one in the preceding paragraph can be tested by asking yourself whether it is true of first-language users. If it is, there is a good chance that the same goes for second-language skills. Do first-language users, as children or adults, have difficulty in giving descriptions, or in telling stories? Is this something which first-language users can usefully practise?

Broadly speaking, information routines may be identified as expository or evaluative. Expository routines are those which involve factual information hinging on questions of sequencing or identity of the subject. Brown and Yule (1983) suggest that the principal types of expository routine are narration, description, and instruction. One way of defining the differences is presented in the chart in Table 1.

	Sequencing	Subject
Narrative	+	+
Description	−	+
Instruction	+	−

Table 1: Features of expository routines
(adapted from Longacre 1983)

▶ TASK 21

Complete the following statements about Table 1.

1 The term _____ is closely related to the time dimension.
2 Sentence subject is of importance in both _Narr_ and _Descr_ .
3 The dimension most closely related to problems of identification is _____ .

4 Narrative and instruction have in common the dimension of
_____ .

5 The subject dimension in instruction is generally expressed by
_____ or _____ .

Evaluative routines are often, if not always, based on expository routines.
They involve the drawing of conclusions, usually requiring the expression
of reasoning. Evaluative routines typically involve explanations; predictions; justifications; preferences and decisions (see Table 2).

Expository routines	*Evaluation routines*
description	explanation
narration	justification
instruction	prediction
comparison	decision

Table 2: Information routines

▶ TASK 22

What do preferences and decisions have in common? White (1979)
suggests that they may both be based on comparisons. Why? In what
way might a prediction require to be supported by some reasoning?

Brown and Yule (1983) take a further step towards defining oral skills,
exemplifying their discussion in relation to narrative. Narrative, they
suggest, consists of a certain number of essential components. These are the
following:

setting
time
participants
event
a point.

In order to manage a story of any kind, the speaker must be able to give an
economical but accurate account of each of these components. One aspect
of the difficulty of such a task is related to the number of elements occurring
under each category. So, for example, a narrative will be more difficult if
there is more than one participant, or if the setting changes during the
story. The time reference may also change. There might be more than one
event which goes to make up the story. There may even be more than one
point to the story.

TASK 23

Brown and Yule point out that descriptions of an accident using toy cars can be made more difficult using these variables. How do you think this might be? How might an evening out be similarly made more difficult to describe?

In order to show how important the number of variables can be, Brown and Yule suggest that a story gets harder to tell if the number of participants is increased in the following ways:

1 one person;
2 one female and one male, or one child and one adult;
3 two of the same sex and age;
4 two of the same sex and age, and one of a different sex or age;
5 three of the same sex and age.

Obviously the list could be considerably extended.

TASK 24

The authors illustrate this by varying the toy vehicles in the traffic accident. How could you make it easier or harder to give an account of an accident using one or more lorries, buses, or cars? Are there any other features of vehicles which could be used to vary the difficulty of the task in a similar way? Consider a description, for instance, of a room; a table; a bowl of fruit. How could these be made easier or harder? How can street directions be made easier or harder?

This aspect of complexity is one way in which the skill of speakers in handling chunks of information can be improved and tested. It is also a dimension of oral skill which is just as central to first-language ability as to second-language ability.

Interaction routines
The second kind of routine is interactional. Interaction routines are routines based not so much on information content as on sequences of kinds of terms occurring in typical kinds of interactions. Routines thus can be characterized in broad terms to include the kinds of turns typically occurring in given situations, and the order in which the components are likely to occur. Thus 'service encounters', telephone conversations, interview situations, casual encounters, conversations at parties, conversations around the table at a dinner party, lessons, radio or television interviews, all tend to be organized in characteristic ways.

▶ TASK 25

To try the native-speaker test, consider whether native speakers have difficulty in any of the following: being interviewed; speaking on the phone; handling restaurant situations; speaking to superiors; making polite conversation with strangers; complaining.

Schank and Abelson (1977), in a well-known example of an interaction routine, argue that although we may not know exactly what words or meanings will be communicated in a restaurant situation, it is still quite easy to predict the kinds of information that will be asked for and given on any visit to a traditional restaurant. What would you expect (a) the client and (b) the waiter to communicate to each other? And how could you divide such an episode into parts? What order would the parts have?

As with informational routines, the proof that interactional routines exist can be found in the fact that speakers can get parts wrong. Thus the organization of routines is not necessarily tightly defined. Rather incompetence can be recognized when one of the speakers is 'brusque', or 'rude', or 'disorganized' because he or she starts talking without producing an initial greeting, or checking who is on the other end of the phone. Good performers, as Scollon and Scollon (1983) point out in relation to job interviews, are those who can meet the expectations of the other parties within the bounds of acceptable convention. Once again, this does not necessarily mean knowing a text off by heart, just knowing what expectations and possibilities can be realized in the given situation.

In so far as politeness conventions are based on common sense, these routines can also be seen as logical. However, the logic followed is based on what it makes sense to say before you go on to say anything else. For example, greetings sensibly come at the beginning of conversations, and farewells at the end. Telephone conversations reasonably enough begin by a check on who the other speaker is. Greetings may or may not include questions about the health of the listener and his or her relatives.

▶ TASK 26

As a further example, requests or reminders are very often preceded by a 'preface'. Farewells are similarly often prepared by what is called a 'preclosing' move. What do you think a preface or preclosing move is? (Consider what it would be like if people simply stopped their conversation, said 'Goodbye' and walked off. Do people suddenly in the middle of a phone call briskly say 'Bye for now' and hang up? What if someone asked for an important favour when it turned out that it was quite out of the question for the other person to help, and yet a refusal was embarrassing? How would it appear?)

As with informational routines, each of these conventions has a certain logic, although conventions may vary from one culture to another.

The point to be made here, then, is that speakers build up a more or less extensive repertoire of routines. These are both informational and interactional and are a product of their familiarity with certain kinds of communication: types of information structure, and types of interactional sequence. Both of these kinds of routine reflect 'categories of knowledge'. They can even become stock patterns or 'patters'. Fillmore (1979) suggests that the patter of a tour guide or entertainer could provide an interesting subject of study. One of the features that learners can hope to acquire, then, is knowledge of this kind. However, learners also need another more general kind of skill, the skill to negotiate specific communicative problems. This is the topic to be considered next.

4.3 Negotiation skills

Apart from the knowledge of routines, there is also the area of skill involved in getting through the routines on specific occasions, so that understanding is achieved. There are two main aspects to this. One involves what might be called the *management of interaction*, and the other consists of the *negotiation of meaning*. Both of these are affected by the fact that the listener is on the spot, and can influence in many ways what shape the interaction takes.

By *negotiation of meaning* we refer to the skill of communicating ideas clearly. This includes the way participants signal understanding during an exchange, and is an aspect of spoken interaction which contrasts most sharply with the position of the reader and writer of the written word. In written discourse, there is nothing that either the reader or the writer can do about the other one's 'mistakes'. The reader cannot alter what the writer writes, and the writer cannot make sure that the reader understands. There is no direct negotiation between the two. This is the first kind of interaction skill we are concerned with.

The second kind of interaction skill, *management of interaction*, refers to the business of agreeing who is going to speak next, and what he or she is going to talk about. Interaction of the kind we are concerned with takes place without a chairperson to decide the order in which people will speak or what can be spoken about. There is no one around to protect the speaking rights of foreign speakers: they have to do this themselves. We will now look briefly at these two aspects of negotiation.

▶ TASK 27

The speakers can negotiate on several levels. For instance they can:

1 influence the level of understanding;
2 try to take control of the conversation;
3 be hostile to the other speaker;
4 interrupt;
5 add information;
6 ask for or give clarification.

At any of these levels, the speaker must take heed of the listener's reaction, otherwise things may go badly wrong. Which of these involve management skills, and which involve negotiation of meaning?

Earlier, we compared normal spoken interaction with the ability to drive a car. The element of negotiation is also present on the road. How can drivers influence each other (a) helpfully; (b) unhelpfully?

Consider the following passage. Are the speakers co-operative? What evidence is there? How could it have been different? What effect do you think a co-operative or unco-operative approach has on the interaction?

Peter: What I've been doing is cutting down on my sleep.
Deborah: Oy! [sighs]
Peter: And I've been . . . and I s
Deborah: I do that too
              but it's painful.
Peter: Yeah. Five, six hours a night,
              and
Deborah: Oh God, how can you do it. You survive?
Peter: Yeah late afternoon meetings are hard. . . . But outside
                    Deborah: mmmm
              of that I can keep going pretty well
Deborah: Not sleeping enough is
              terrible . . . I'd much rather not eat than not sleep.
Peter: I probably should not eat so much, it would . . . it
              would uh . . . save a lot of time.
Deborah: If I'm like really busy I don't I don't I don't eat
              I don't yeah I just don't eat but I
Peter: I I tend to
              spend a lot of time eating and preparing and
Deborah: Oh: I
              never prepare food . . . I eat whatever I can get my
              hands on.
Peter: Yeah.
(Tannen 1984:82–3)

4.4 Negotiation of meaning

There are several aspects to negotiation of meaning. In what follows we are going to concentrate particularly on the negotiation of meaning in the sense of making oneself understood. Widdowson uses the term 'convergence' here, to indicate that what is involved is mutual understanding rather than individual understanding.

Here once again we have a major difference between written and spoken language: in spoken language, understanding is assumed to have taken place by the end of a conversation unless it has been shown to be otherwise. Because of this, the speakers during the communication are in a position to ensure understanding. In written communication things are different: in writing, communication is the affair of the participants taken individually. In speaking, on the other hand, negotiation of meaning is a mutual concern.

In order to ensure understanding, there are two important factors. First of all, there is the question of choosing a level of explicitness and detail which we think is appropriate to our interlocutor. The second factor concerns the procedures used for ensuring understanding. First, then, the problem of selecting the appropriate level of explicitness.

Level of explicitness

The first aspect of negotiation concerns what we call *level of explicitness*. By this we are referring to the speaker's choices of expression in the light of what our interlocutor knows, what he or she needs to know or can understand.

▶ ## TASK 28

It is no good speaking about our house to someone who does not know it in the same way as we would to someone who knows it well. The same is true of virtually any subject: we adjust what we say according to whom we are speaking to. The problem of level of explicitness is one of taking into consideration what the listener knows and what he or she can understand. The listener wants neither too much information, nor too little.

Consider the following situation. You have invited some friends to your place for a party. At one point, you need a bottle opener but, because many of your guests happen to be chatting in the kitchen, you are unable to get to the drawer where it is kept. In the following examples, in one case you are speaking to your spouse, in another to a close friend, in another to a friend who has never been to your house, and in one to a foreign visitor. Which of the requests is addressed to which person?

1 **You**: Could you get me a bottle opener out of the drawer in the table please?

2 **You**: Do you think you could get me a bottle opener? You'll find one in a drawer which is situated at the other end of the table.

3 **You**: Bottle opener, please.

4 **You**: I need something to open this bottle with. Could you get something for me? If you go to the other end of the table you will find a drawer. If you open the drawer you should find a bottle opener. Would you mind?

What features of the language can you see as evidence to support your choice?

The problem is that as foreign-language users, we generally proceed on the assumption that understanding between native speakers is always perfect, and that problems of misunderstanding arise only because we are not native speakers. Of course, our own experience of the first language belies this. For example, limitations on understanding can be a source of conflict between generations. Foreign-language learners seem to forget this. When entering a foreign-language community, we may well imagine that we alone are approximate in our level of communication: that all the native speakers function normally by producing all their messages in a complete and self-sufficient manner, which will be perfectly comprehensible to all hearers.

In fact, perfectly explicit communication, as we well know, is not only generally unattainable, it is also generally unnecessary. However, by imagining that it is possible and necessary, foreign-language learners may be making things more difficult for themselves than they need. The important point, then, is that the degree of explicitness necessary for a given message may vary according to the person one is talking to.

▶ # TASK 29

Consider the following exchange between husband and wife:

Wife: Did you ring, then?
Husband: Yes, Friday.
Wife: Good, a risotto OK?
Husband: Fine.

What are they talking about? How do they know? How do you know? Should they be more explicit?

Here is an example from Act 1 of Harold Pinter's play *The Birthday Party*. What is the effect here?

Stanley (*advancing*): They're coming today.
Meg: Who?
Stanley: They're coming in a van.
Meg: Who?

Stanley: And do you know what they've got in that van?
Meg: What?
Stanley: They've got a wheelbarrow in that van.
Meg: (*breathlessly*): They haven't.
Stanley: Oh yes they have.
Meg: You're a liar [. . .]
Stanley: They're looking for someone.
Meg: They're not.
Stanley: They're looking for someone, a certain person.
Meg: (*hoarsely*): No, they're not!
Stanley: Shall I tell you who they're looking for?
Meg: No!
Stanley: You don't want me to tell you?
Meg: You're a liar.

Stanley is using the same linguistic device as the husband and wife in the previous dialogue. It is known as *innuendo*. But Stanley is using it in a threatening way: suggesting danger without stating it.

Unlike Stanley, what we normally do as speakers is to aim for a *sufficient* level of understanding. We do not normally withhold information deliberately in conversation. This is consistent with Grice's co-operative principle of quantity:

> Make your contribution just as informative as required.
> (Grice, 1975)

If you do not say enough, the risk is obvious. However, there is also the opposite risk, that of being too explicit. It is not co-operative to give too much information, or to insist on excessive detail. What is the effect of this?

 ## TASK 30

Explicitness can always be pushed a bit further, yet this is not usually normal. In *The Birthday Party*, we find the following example. What is abnormal here?

Stanley: What's it like out today?
Petey: Very nice.
Stanley: Warm?
Petey: Well, there's a good breeze blowing.
Stanley: Cold?
Petey: No, no, I wouldn't say it was cold.

Lack of explicitness may appear arrogant and aggressive; perhaps obscure and pretentious, and certainly very often unco-operative. It tends to leave the listener feeling that he has too much work to do, or else that the speaker does not care about getting his message across. The second type of problem—that of too much explicitness—leaves the listener with too much redundant language to process, too much detail, or else he finds himself under interrogation. As a consequence, he may feel bored, provoked, or confused.

▶ # TASK 31

In what ways can non-native speakers be:

a. insufficiently explicit?
b. too explicit?

In what ways can this occur with native speakers speaking to non-native speakers?

In each case, which do you think may be the greater problem, (a) or (b)? In your opinion, what is the reason for this?

To find the right level, speakers have to predict, often guessing what their interlocutors know. As speakers, we generally have to assume a lot of all kinds of knowledge. We only add more if our listener indicates that this is necessary. We work towards convergence by saying something, and being prepared to reformulate our message if what we say turns out to have been misunderstood. Even first-language users can have difficulty in doing this successfully.

Procedures of negotiation
The second aspect of the negotiation of meaning that is relevant here concerns the procedures which speakers follow to ensure that understanding takes place. What we have been discussing so far is the level of background explicitness. How much background knowledge can be assumed by the speaker? This is very important in whatever we have to say. However, another aspect of our explicitness affects the words and phrases we choose when we speak. Negotiation of meaning concerns not only how much information is communicated, but also how specific we are in what we say.

This can involve various strategies of communication that we are all very familiar with. For example, it includes paraphrase, metaphor, and the use of vocabulary to vary the degree of precision with which we communicate. As we have seen, in many circumstances it is sufficient to use a general term and modify its precision if this should turn out to be necessary. At other times, however, we are more careful with our first choice of term, because we wish to avoid some stereotyped thought pattern. We consequently make a point of using words more carefully, choosing a metaphor or a paraphrase to emphasize a particular aspect of a message, its seriousness or its humour.

▶ TASK 32

Consider, for instance, the procedures used for providing a definition. These may include different types of syntax typically used for defining, and specific strategies. What phrases are typically used for definitions? How do speakers typically construct and formulate definitions? Here are two examples: 'For instance, a kangaroo is a marsupial'; 'to criticize is for instance when you say to someone "I don't like the way you speak with your mouth full"'.

Paribakht (1985) provides many examples of the types of strategy that learners use to put across meanings which they think they do not know the word for. The ability to mobilize such expressions rapidly is clearly a language skill which both native and non-native speakers can find very useful.

A particularly important set of procedures are those of the necessary conversational adjustments which speakers continually have to make in order to maintain contact with each other and ensure understanding. When people speak to each other, it is thought that they draw on knowledge of the way such exchanges typically proceed in order to be able to deal with problems as and when they arise. This is probably very useful for learners. Knowledge of various ways of getting things repeated, or clarified, or indeed how to repeat and clarify things themselves, is likely to be highly useful.

▶ TASK 33

Consider the situation you are in when someone stops you in the street to ask you the way to one of the main roads in the town. Since you don't know your interlocutor, you may start like this: *Do you know the town?* To which the stranger replies: *No.* Now you know roughly the scale of the problem. You will assume quite a lot of common knowledge—referred to as *schematic* knowledge—such as what traffic lights are and what they look like, and even what prominent landmarks are likely to look like (post offices and banks, for instance, tend to have a predictable appearance within a given country). What you have to do is to provide enough information for the stranger to find her way, using the general knowledge that you expect her to have.

However, what if the stranger says she does know the town? How do you think you might reply? What techniques are you likely to use?

Finally, what if you are the stranger and you not only do not know the town, but you come from abroad? What problems might ensue? Try filling in the blanks in the following dialogue. What do you find yourself doing?

Local: Oh, it's where the Fox and Hounds is.
You: _____
Local: Ah, well, you know the Market? Well, it's there, just next to the Market, on the right.
You: _____
Local: Oh, you don't come from here, I see, well now let's see, you need to go past the Park Gates, turn right and . . .
You: _____
Local: The Park Gates? Straight ahead.
You: _____
Local: Keep going along here and when you get to the lights, ask again.

Once the participants begin a conversation, the *reciprocal* nature of the interaction is an important dimension. This is because it is a condition of most talk that the reactions of the listener affect what is being said. Talk is addressed directly to someone, and whoever has the role of listener is expected to reply immediately. This requires the ability to adapt what one says to what has just gone before, to produce and tailor language smoothly and readily—it involves improvisation. This is very different from what tends to go on in written communication or formal talks.

What is characteristic of interaction routines? There are a certain number of features which are relevant here. All involve 'feedback': that is, the business of checking understanding as the interaction unfolds. From the speaker's point of view, they include the following:

announcing or indicating one's purpose in advance;
indicating friendliness;
checking that the other person has understood;
asking the other person for information or language that he or she has
    forgotten;
asking the other person's opinion;
responding to requests for clarification from the listener(s), for instance by
    rephrasing, repeating, giving example or analogies;
checking common ground;
adapting to points made by the interlocutor;
clarifying meaning or intention by summarizing.

From the listener's point of view, there is a similar set of responses which complement the preceding ones:

indicating understanding by gestures, facial expression, or markers as the
    speaker proceeds;
checking or indicating understanding by summarizing the speaker's
    meaning or intention;
indicating uncertainty about comprehension;
indicating incomprehension;
asking for clarification;

indicating current interpretations;

expressing appropriate agreement, reservations or appreciation of speaker's point;

interrupting where necessary to express any of the foregoing.

For a non-native speaker, these may be important in all kinds of spoken interaction. The ability to think on one's feet in this way may be a common enough skill in one's first language, although one which native speakers do not necessarily share equally in all circumstances. In a second language, however, it is an ability which does not come simply through learning the vocabulary. Difficulty in responding can give the impression that the non-native speaker is rather stiff, formal, or slow. It is important for the development of speech skills, therefore, for learners to have practice in handling routine types of interaction.

These might include:

formal committee-type meetings;
public meetings;
debates;
informal chat with a friend;
service encounters;
social interaction;
oral presentations;
informal discussion;
informal planning and decision-making;
game-playing.

The ability to handle interaction routines in these various types of circumstances clearly requires practice; and such practice clearly depends on the provision of activities which will require learners to become used to dealing with the kinds of unpredictable problems which reciprocal speech brings in each of these interaction situations.

This might help foreign-language learners to develop the skill of negotiating satisfactory mutual understanding in two general ways. For one thing they may thus get used to the feeling of not always communicating exactly what they intend, and working towards as close an approximation as they can. For another, they may get into the habit of asking more often for clarification, which is useful when a lack of experience of the language can make it difficult to understand clearly the intentions of other speakers.

4.5 Management of interaction

Interaction management groups together the kind of freedom participants have which distinguishes a conversation from a meeting or a lecture. Both participants can intervene as and when they wish. They can exercise their rights over many aspects of the interaction directly, and without the intervention of anyone else (such as a chairperson).

Interaction management has at least two aspects: firstly agenda management, and secondly turn-taking. The first refers essentially to control over the content, that is, the choice of topic of an exchange, while turn-taking relates to the obvious aspect of who speaks when and for how long.

Agenda management

Agenda management essentially covers the participants' right to choose the topic and the way the topics are developed, and to choose how long the conversation should continue. Here then we are concerned with the basic freedom to start, maintain, direct, and end a conversation without conforming to a script, and without the intervention of a third party.

Brown and Yule (1983) describe how social talk creates a characteristic structure in the resulting conversation:

> People meeting on the bus or train for the very first time, people meeting at parties, people meeting at the beginning of a new lecture course will tend to conduct a type of talk where *one person offers a topic for comment by the other person, responds to the other person if his topic is successful, and if it is not, proffers another topic of conversation.* Such primarily interactional chats *are frequently characterised by constantly shifting topics and a great deal of agreement on them.*
> (1983:11, my italics)

The structure of socially-orientated conversation is smoother, quicker, and less concerned with detail. Brown and Yule point out that in a typical piece of conversation, even if it is short conversation, the topics will shift a lot. Consequently, topic selection may be far freer and change more frequently and more spontaneously in social talk than in more institutional talk. This is undoubtedly a potential source of trouble for unpractised non-native speakers.

▶ TASK 34

The business of what topic is to be spoken about is partly a matter of the interest of the participants, and partly a matter of what is appropriate in given circumstances. There are, however, skills connected with topics which may be important for speakers. These include knowing how to bring up an initial topic; to develop a topic; to bring in a new topic as an extension of the previous one; to switch topic; to open or close a conversation.

In the following extracts are there any examples of topic change? Do they cause any problems?

a. **Steve:** Cause they were built near the swamp . . . We used to go . . . hunting frogs in the swamps.
Deborah: Where was it. Where were yours?
Steve: In the Bronx.
Peter: In the Bronx. In the East Bronx?
Deborah: How long did you live in it?
Steve: Near the swamps? . . . Now there's a big co-operative building.
Peter: Three years.
Deborah: Three years?
(Tannen 1984:67)

Consider this from the point of view of Chad, who has just been asked about a trip he made to New York. The conversation proceeds quite briskly.

b. **Chad:** That's what I expected to find in New York was lots of bagels.
David: Yeah lots of bagels and when you go to Boston you expect to find beans
Steve: Did you find them?
Chad: No, no. What I found were were uh: . . . croisuh crescent rolls? and croissant? and all that? . . . the . . . crescent rolls mostly. Lots of that kind of stuff. But it was
Steve: Where?
David: Croissant.
Chad: I don't know . . . I didn't go round a whole lot for breakfast. I was kind of . . . stuck in . . . the Plaza for a while which was interesting.
Deborah: You stayed at the Plaza?
Chad: Yeah.
Deborah: Hoooooooooooo!
Steve: Were you on the West side at all?
(Tannen 1984:68)

Do you know of any teaching materials which provide any opportunity to practise negotiating one's topic?

Drama once again provides examples of the problems in choosing the topic of one's next turn. Take this extract from Act 1 of *The Birthday Party*.

Lulu: Hasn't Mrs Boles got enough to do without having you under her feet all day?
Stanley: I always stand on the table when she sweeps the floor.
Lulu: Why don't you have a wash? You look terrible.
Stanley: A wash wouldn't make any difference.

Lulu   (*rising*): Come out and get a bit of air. You depress me,
       looking like that.
Stanley: Air? Oh, I don't know about that.
Lulu: It's lovely out. And I've got a few sandwiches.
Stanley: What sort of sandwiches?
Lulu: Cheese.
Stanley: I'm a big eater, you know.
Lulu: That's all right. I'm not hungry.

Part of the problem in oral interaction is ensuring a coherent response in the short amount of time available. An appropriate utterance has to be mobilized in response to the immediately preceding utterance. Pinter's play offers many examples of short four- or six-line exchanges which illustrate this. You might imagine you are Lulu in the first extract, and then McCann in the other. What would *you* say?

Stanley   (*abruptly*): How would you like to go away with me?
Lulu: Where?
Stanley: Nowhere. Still, we could go.
Lulu: But where could we go?
Stanley: Nowhere. There's nowhere to go. So we could just go.
          It wouldn't matter.
Lulu: We might as well stay here.
Stanley: No. It's no good here.
Lulu: Well, where else is there?
Stanley: Nowhere.
Lulu: Well, that's a charming proposal.   (Act 1)

McCann: Were you going out?
Stanley: Yes.
McCann: On your birthday?
Stanley: Yes, why not?
McCann: But they're holding a party here for you tonight.
Stanley: Oh Really? That's unfortunate.
McCann: Ah no. It's very nice.
                                                      (Act 2)

It is noticeable that there is nothing structurally or philosophically complex about the dialogues. However, they are like short sharp duels, and many native speakers would find it hard to manage such speed and agility of response, particularly with strangers (McCann and Stanley are not close acquaintances).

▶ TASK 35

In what sorts of circumstances do speakers have greatest freedom of choice of topic: in professional or social situations? Why? What sorts of topic sequences might be appropriate at a first social encounter at a party; in a telephone call to a friend to invite him to dinner; in a telephone call to a friend to ask about a professional matter; in a call to your school director to ask for an appointment to meet her?

Turn-taking

The second way in which a speaker of a foreign language needs to know how to negotiate control of a conversation is through the business of handling *turn-taking*. The speaker has to be efficient at getting a turn and to be good at letting another speaker have a turn. Let's look at what this consists of.

Efficient turn-taking requires five abilities. First it involves knowing how to signal that one wants to speak, by using appropriate phrases or sounds, or even gestures. Some devices can be very useful to get one's point in. An example would be that of starting one's turn by initially agreeing in some way with the previous speaker, before moving on to make a slightly—or completely—different point.

Second, it means recognizing the right moment to get a turn. An interruption at the wrong moment can sound very rude, but at other moments it is acceptable. Thirdly, it is important to know how to use appropriate turn structure in order to use one's turn properly and not lose it before finishing what one has to say. Gumperz (1982), for instance, reports that speakers of some cultures expect to be allowed to preface their turn with a lengthy background explanation before getting to the point. Other cultures may have different conventions, and expect the speaker to get to the point more quickly. Fourthly, one has to be able to recognize other people's signals of their desire to speak. And fifthly, one needs to know how to let someone else have a turn.

▶ ## TASK 36

Turn-taking involves making various decisions about how and when to say something during a conversation, and how long to go on for. Consider the materials you use. Do they provide learners with activities which require this kind of decision-making? You might try to find examples of how such activities proceed.

It has been suggested that a learner gets sufficient oral practice by listening to the teacher speaking to, or interacting with, the whole class. Consider the following extract from a lesson. Which of the five aspects of turn-taking identified above can learners develop here?

> T(eacher): Where does it go before it reaches your lungs?
> P(upil): Your windpipe, Miss.
> T: Down your windpipe . . . Now can anyone remember the other word for windpipe?
> P: The trachea.

T: The trachea . . . good . . . After it has gone to the trachea where does it go to then? . . . There are a lot of little pipes going into the lungs . . . what are those called? Ian?

P: The bronchii.

T: The bronchii . . . that's the plural . . . what's the singular? What is one of these tubes called? Ann?

P: Bronchus.

T: Bronchus . . . with 'us' at the end . . . What does inspiration mean . . .?

(from Barnes 1969, quoted in Coulthard 1985)

Consider the speaker describing the traffic accident in Task 18. At what points might a listener make a contribution? What kind of contribution, and why?

It may seem that this is all very obvious. However, it is noticeable that first-language speakers are not all equally good at doing this. Some find it very hard to get a turn, and others find it very hard to allow others a chance to speak (see Tannen 1984). In either case, the problem for a speaker of a first language can be quite serious: it might make it very difficult for him or her to get a job or function efficiently at work; it might also make it very difficult to get or keep friends.

▶ **TASK 37**

Consider speaking on the telephone or at a meeting. Do people have difficulties in speaking in these situations? Why do you think problems can arise? Do people ever find themselves speaking out of turn, or interrupting, when this is something they never do in private? Can it be a first-language problem?

Listen to a television or radio panel discussion. Note difficulties that speakers may have in getting a turn: do speakers fail to get turns; do speakers interrupt each other apparently impolitely; do speakers interrupt each other with special formulas to smooth the way; do speakers signal that they want to have a turn without getting one; do speakers get a turn only after many signals? How do speakers keep turns?

If this can be a problem for first-language users, there are even firmer grounds for thinking that the problem is more acute for speakers of a foreign language. After all, they are preparing for spoken contact with people of a different background who will not always know what they intend to say unless they claim their speaking rights for themselves.

4.6 Conclusion

Each of these aspects of negotiation is an important component of first-language ability. An individual's control of them can have a considerable effect on his or her public and private life. People functioning in a foreign language, in a culture to which they are not accustomed, also hope to be able to operate as intelligent and efficient individuals. If they have the ability to understand and handle these aspects of oral language, then they are more likely to be confident speakers of the foreign language. They are also more likely to be confident *learners of the foreign language*.

What we have been looking at here are some of the decisions that speakers have to make, and negotiate, with their interlocutors. They may be useful for organizing our classrooms, for developing oral activities, and for evaluating our learners' performance. If negotiation skills are important, then they surely need to be practised in learning tasks.

5   Learner strategies of communication

NS: . . . how do you get on with girls—
L: oh (giggles) I'm very oh—what do you call it—you know
      (laughs) I get a red in my head—(giggles)
NS: yes shy
L: shy yer
(from Færch and Kasper 1983:223)

5.1 Introduction

So far the discussion has been about the nature of spoken interaction as
realized by first-language users. But how do learners cope? Although we
may have an understanding of certain important aspects of oral
communication, as teachers we must also be concerned to find out how oral
skills are learnt. In what follows we shall look at how learners
communicate when they have not mastered the language. This means
discussing learners' strategies of oral communication.

Studies of learners' communication strategies have examined the ways
learners deal with communication problems. Færch and Kasper (1983)
contains several articles which discuss this. Communication strategies
identified include the following:

A. Achievement strategies:
    1 Guessing strategies
    2 Paraphrase strategies
    3 Co-operative strategies

B. Reduction strategies:
    1 Avoidance strategies . . .

First, the difference between achievement strategies and reduction
strategies. Both these types of strategy aim to compensate for a problem of
expression. The learner anticipates a difficulty in expressing what she
intended—indeed the difficulty may have been explicitly signalled by the
interlocutor, who has not understood the speaker's first attempt. What
does the speaker do?

If she uses an *achievement strategy*, she will attempt to compensate for her
language gap by improvising a substitute. This involves attempting to find a
way of conveying her message, often by guess-work, intuition, 'feel', an
expression she thinks she remembers, or various kinds of analogy.

▶ TASK 38

One example of an achievement strategy is as follows:

L: I came down from twenty degrees—er I don't know
      how you say twe it was *twenty degrees hot* you know
NS: mm
L: and I came up er in Scotland to *twenty degrees freezing*
      so I got very sick just before Christmas.
(from Haastrup and Phillipson 1983:149)

The learner uses the two expressions indicated by italics instead of
plus twenty/minus twenty, or *twenty above/below zero*. The point is
that the learner has thought up expressions which serve his purpose
quite well, even though they are not the normal native-speaker
choice. He has got out of his vocabulary difficulty by improvising an
alternative. Would you agree that his strategy achieves his intended
aim?

In using achievement strategies, then, speakers do not lose or alter any of
their message. However, they may not be able to use an achievement
strategy; instead they may have to adopt a *reduction strategy*. For instance,
they may manage only a partial solution and so fail to communicate all of
their intended message. Or else, they may find no solution at all. In either
case, the result is that they reduce their message so as either to bring it
within the scope of their knowledge or else to abandon that message and go
on to something they can manage. Both of these solutions have been called
reduction strategies.

Reduction strategies must presumably be very widespread, since the
business of speaking without a full repertoire of foreign-language
expressions must often result in loss of message content, particularly in the
early stages. During communication this can take many forms. One such is
the following:

L: I have to look after a machine if something is er doesn't work I
      have to well it's not difficult because there's only three buttons
      you know all automatical
(Haastrup and Phillipson 1983:150)

In this extract the speaker is supposed to be describing his job in a laundry.
However, when he gets down to saying what he has to do with the machine,
he abandons his attempt, changes direction and talks about the controls. By
keeping his talk within the bounds of what he is able to say, the speaker
manages to maintain production and fluency.

We will now look a little more closely at the forms these strategies can take.

5.2 Achievement strategies

1 We have called the first of the achievement strategies *guessing*. In discussion of reading skills (for example, Smith 1978), much is made of intelligent guessing; but guessing occurs just as much in oral production (in a sense, what we said about explicitness in Unit 4 implied a lot of meaningful guessing). There are several kinds of 'guessing' strategy. If a speaker uses 'guessing' strategies, he probes for a word which he does not know or is not sure of, using his knowledge of the morphology of the language. He hopes that he'll hit on a word or expression which his interlocutor will recognize and understand.

There are various types of guessing strategy he might use.

a. He can *foreignize* a mother-tongue word, pronouncing it as though it belonged to the target language (a Frenchman speaking English might be pleased with the results if he foreignized the French word 'manoeuvre'; a German native-speaker might have less success if he produced the form 'manikin' to mean 'little man').

b. He might more simply *borrow* a word from his mother tongue, without changing it in any way, hoping perhaps that his interlocutor will recognize it (for example, an English speaker saying 'Il y a deux *candles* sur la cheminée' (from Bialystok 1983:105)).

c. Alternatively, he can provide a *literal translation* of his mother-tongue word (a Frenchman may attempt to say 'crescent' instead of 'croissant' and fail to be understood; a Portuguese speaker could try 'feast' instead of 'party' or 'holiday', based on 'festa').

d. A fourth guessing strategy he might use is to *coin* a word: he can invent a target-language word creatively on the basis of his knowledge of the language, hoping that the interlocutor once again will get the idea (for example *airball* for 'balloon' (from Tarone 1983:62)). In this way he might even produce a suitable target-language cognate or borrowed word which he had not realized existed in the target language (for instance an English speaker might produce the verb *flipper* which can be used to mean 'go insane').

2 Instead of one of these guessing strategies, he can use a *paraphrase strategy*. This basically involves searching his knowledge of the target-language vocabulary to find an alternative to the expression that he needs. He can do this broadly in one of two ways. One thing he can do is to look for some kind of vocabulary item—say a synonym or a more general word. This we might call a *lexical substitution strategy*. Alternatively, he can try to assemble some sort of phrase to explain his concept. This we might call *circumlocution*.

If he looks for a synonym or a more general word (called a 'superordinate'—'animal' is superordinate for 'gerbil' or 'mongoose' or 'dog') then perhaps no one will notice that he didn't know a word. For example, talking about a man at an airport, a student said: 'yeah . but that may be er a *customer* . who is in a hurry he is about to . he is about to to *lose* his er . . his aeroplane'. The learner finds rough synonyms to carry his meaning.

However, sometimes the word will be too general. For instance, it would sound odd to try to compliment someone on their pet afghan hound by saying 'I like your animal'. On the other hand, sometimes it is not precise enough. For instance, 'It's on the piece of furniture' may not help someone find a purse they are looking for. To compensate for the loss of information with the more general word, we may find ourselves adding a circumlocution: 'It's on the bit of furniture over by the window'.

If he uses circumlocution, the speaker is simply going to express his meaning in several words instead of the one he intended. For example:

> it has waste basket . it has a basket *who probably serves for buying things in the market* = 'a shopping basket';
>
> *a mixing of beige and brown* = 'light brown';
>
> some brushes – – that . *probably they are using them for – for – – – for – – – keeping their clothes . without dust* = 'clothes brushes'.

A lot of what we say in a foreign language may well appear to be circumlocution to native speakers, because we do not always know or recall at the moment of speaking the normal expression:

> *the stairs are also with rugs*—with brown rugs—and there is also a telephone—*t'colour of this telephone is black.*

The speaker undoubtedly knew how to use 'there is/are', and could say 'this telephone is black'. For various reasons, at the moment of putting the ideas into words, the encoding was rather different from what a native speaker might expect. (The same speaker a few minutes later said: 'this bear it has a brown colour'.)

▶ TASK 39

In the following example, what would a native speaker normally have said?

> *my picture's rug is brown*

Would the strategy work?

In the example in Task 39, there would have been no point in teaching the speaker the normal expression: she knew it perfectly well. What she was doing was putting ideas directly into words, paraphrasing or circumlocuting as she attempted to concentrate on her meaning.

3 A third type of achievement strategy that has been identified is what has been called *co-operative strategies*. These are used when the speaker gets help. For instance, he may ask for the word, by asking for a translation of his mother-tongue word, by physically indicating the object that he means,

or by miming. However, he can get help through other means. He may try to provide a syntactic frame in order to elicit the word he wants from his interlocutor.

S1: this little boy is wearing short pants[mhm] and a plaaaiin
S2: shirt

Sometimes co-operation takes place as the two speakers construct the sentence jointly:

S4: you have a basket for
S3: a basket for
S4: for umbrellas
S3: for
S4: umbrellas

▶ **TASK 40**

In the following extracts (taken from Bygate (unpub.)) the two speakers are describing two pictures which are part of a picture story about a street accident. Read through the transcript, and observe any features which could be described as *communication strategies*. What types of strategies do you think they are?

S1: I er in—my picture I have er—erm—it shows—that er there is an accident—erm—a big truck—full of er—er—mercancy—erm—shot er—shoot shooted—a man who is er on the street—er—seems erm—that he he was in a driving a—bicycle—and another one is eh—going to help him—

S2: in my picture I see erm I see a fellow riding a bike[mhm] and er approaching to a corner [mhm] where we can see a truck—it seems to me that th this fellow is not er looking . is not looking at the truck which is er approaching the corner
S1: mhm he must be thinking in something else maybe
S2: yeah maybe
S1:   distracted
S2:   because he's just er looking at looking at the road he's [mm] er bending well this is ah a racing bike [yes] but er besides that he is I just looking down . looking down at the road but not looking before him [mhm]

  S1: they are carrying a man—in ahm—erm—in a portable bed—the one that the hospitals use to carry people that got an accident—and they're taking him—ah from the—from the road—he was on the road—OK but they have just come because—a man—has called the police I mean the the people in charge of looking for these people that have had accidents—right—so actually in the picture the there are two policemen—and the man who telephoned—the hospital

5.3 Reduction strategies

As we have seen, reduction strategies generally involve speakers in reducing their communicative objectives.

Avoidance strategies involve altering one's message in order to keep out of trouble. There are various kinds of trouble one might want to avoid. A learner may want to avoid producing a particular sound sequence (for example, 'tr' or 'th' in English, or the 'euil' or repeated 'r' sounds in French, the nasal 'ão' in Portuguese, or the 'ch' in German).

Alternatively, the learner might want to avoid some tricky structure, for instance, one which will lead towards an impending subjunctive (in French, German, Spanish, or Portuguese); or she may wish to avoid a conditional in English. She may avoid a word whose gender she is unsure of. In these cases, the learner is likely to use an alternative word, and may thus sacrifice part of her intended meaning.

Finally, the learner may simply wish to avoid difficulties in expressing an idea through lack of vocabulary. In this case, she is likely to avoid some message content. One thing she can do is abandon the message, and look for something else to talk about, or even fall silent.

However, instead of avoiding the problem, the learner may rather alter the message so as to make it more manageable. For instance, she may avoid making a technical point: she may confine herself to something more general. Instead of complimenting someone on their house, she may simply thank them for an enjoyable evening. Or say how much she enjoyed the meal, rather than get involved in trying to say how much she appreciated a specific dish whose name, and contents, she cannot pronounce. These are the four main types of communication strategy which have been identified. This has been called 'meaning replacement' (Færch and Kasper 1983:52).

▶ ## TASK 41

Here is another pair of students talking about the same pictures as in the previous examples. This illustrates the possible scope of reduction strategies:

S1: ahm—a man—driving a bicycle—and he is arriving—to the longer street—but erm—in that road there is—a car—a truck—is begin to grows (?)—there—OK

S2: mhm—ahm—ts—number two is on the table [I suppose] yeah number two is on the table—it's ah the man is starting to ride the bicycle—and then a truck is—passing by—and hits—the bicycle.

What we have been discussing here have been called *compensatory strategies*. The learner is dealing with difficulties of *expression*. However, as we have already seen, the learner also has to deal with other problems of communication. For instance, he needs to be able to organize his turns so that he gives himself time to think, time to find his words, and produce a suitable reply. One way to do this is to repeat a part of the previous utterance before producing his own. Another strategy may be to use items from what his interlocutor has said. These may be useful strategies, which enable the learner to find his way about in the language.

He may also find it difficult to carry on long turns, so he may need to develop a way of showing his interest and his good intentions, without speaking as much as he would like. It has been pointed out that native speakers tend to help learners to speak by asking them a lot of questions, so that the learner avoids having to produce much of the conversation (Long 1983). However, it may also be a learner strategy at some point to ask questions himself in order to shift some of the conversational burden. If he fails to understand, he himself can choose when to ask questions for clarification.

▶ ## TASK 42

Considering this discussion of learners' oral communication strategies, what kinds of strategies mentioned seem to you to be the most likely to be of use or importance in the understanding of the learning and teaching of oral skills? Are there any other kinds which you think might be important?

In this unit, we have been looking at some of the strategies which learners use in order to become competent users of the foreign language. An understanding of these features of learners' attempts to cope may improve our perception of the learning process and so enable us to follow learners' progress more closely.

6 A checklist of skills

> Consider [. . .] what is involved in producing a conversational utterance. Apart from being grammatical, the utterance must also be appropriate on very many levels at the same time; it must conform to the speaker's aim, to the role relationships between the interactants, to the setting, topic, linguistic context, etc. The speaker must also produce his utterance within severe constraints; he does not know in advance what will be said to him (and hence what his utterance will be a response to) yet, if the conversation is not to flag, he must respond extremely quickly. The rapid formulation of utterances which are simultaneously 'right' on several levels is central to the (spoken) communicative skill.
> (Johnson 1981:11)

In Unit 1 we began by making a distinction between language knowledge and language skill. The former was described as basically a set of grammar and pronunciation rules, vocabulary, and knowledge about how they are normally used. Skill was seen as the ability to use them. We then suggested that language skill itself can be seen to be of two sorts. Firstly it is the ability to manipulate grammar and vocabulary, and pronounce it correctly. Beyond this, however, oral language is not just written language spoken. Speech involves the use of production skills, notably facilitation and compensation devices. It also involves the skill of resolving specific kinds of communication problems. These are firstly the negotiation of meaning (explicitness and procedures), and secondly the management of interaction (turn-taking and agenda management). These distinctions are shown in the diagram in Figure 1.

There are two features to the diagram. Firstly, skills are dependent on some appropriate knowledge resource. They involve using known conventions for communicating specific meanings. The exercise of the skills, however, can increase the knowledge store. For example, production tricks, once discovered, can be stored as routines. Similarly, ways of structuring a narration can be stored as routines. This knowledge is not raw. It has been handled and processed in one context or another by skills.

The second aspect of the diagram is that the skills are interdependent. They consist of decision-making processes for deciding on messages, formulating them, and executing them, all while monitoring the state of play. The spoken skill, taken as a whole, involves the ability to handle all the sub-skills from the top of the diagram to the bottom. In other words, accuracy skills on their own are not sufficient.

As negotiation routines are invented and repeated and refined by the user, they are likely to be stored in the memory as the speaker finds them useful or successful. Such knowledge is accumulated through working with the language in specific contexts in order to do specific tasks. So this area of knowledge may well *depend* for its growth and improvement on the use and development of interaction skills.

In the next section, we will be looking at various views of the methodology of teaching oral language ability, and the kinds of activities that can be best used to help these oral skills to develop.

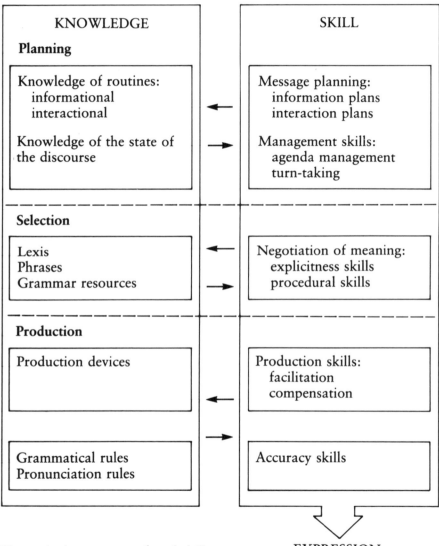

Figure 1: A summary of oral skills   EXPRESSION

The methodology
of oral interaction

7 Introduction

In Section One we discussed the major aspects of oral language skills. These were summarized in Unit 6. Having identified potential teaching objectives, we now need to consider how these objectives can be attained. In this section we have four aims:

1 to consider the methodology of teaching oral skills;
2 to assess some actual examples of oral materials;
3 to consider the language of learners working on such activities;
4 to discuss the place of oral skills in the curriculum.

These questions will be approached in the light of points raised in Section One. First it might be useful to clarify these aims.

In this section, we are concerned with how oral skills can be taught and learnt. This involves thinking about objectives (see Unit 8), and types of oral activities (see Unit 9). Since most discussion has in the past been devoted to materials for developing accuracy skills, it seemed more important in this book to concentrate mainly on interaction activities, basing the discussion on Units 3, 4, and 6. Some discussion of proposals for accuracy tasks is included, however, and references are included for further information in the bibliography at the end of the book.

Our second aim in this section is to assess some examples of oral materials (see Unit 10). For this we will refer to our summary of the features of oral skills presented in Unit 6. We will be wanting to assess how far these features are realized by the activities available, and which, if any, are not.

Our third main objective in this section is to begin some kind of assessment of learners' performance when they are given interaction tasks to perform (see Unit 11). This is based partly on our outline in Unit 6, and partly on our discussion of learner strategies in Unit 5. While it is important to apply methodological theory in the form of specific activities, it is also useful to attempt to understand the results of the use of such materials. Classroom decisions, and the theories they are based on, can thus be evaluated in the light of outcomes.

▶ TASK 43

This, of course, is analogous with many other professions, for instance the evaluation of the outcomes of medical decisions. What evaluation would you expect the medical profession to be interested in with respect to:

1 the growth and illnesses of a child;
2 therapy aimed at helping a physically handicapped invalid?

In what other professions would you expect research to evaluate the results of professional decisions?

By scrutinizing learner output we are in a position to form a clearer understanding of how learners may progress, and how they may differ. Finally, we consider the more general proposals of methodologists regarding the place of oral activities in language-learning programmes (Unit 12). These include such questions as the place of oral activities in relation to the development of other skills, and the position of interaction skills in relation to accuracy skills and language knowledge. We will be mainly concerned with the suggestions regarding the role of interaction skills in relation to the development of accuracy skills (Unit 12). This is based mainly on the distinction made in Unit 1 between accuracy and interaction skills.

8   Oral skills: methodological objectives

8.1 Introduction

In methodology, there are two central questions. Firstly, what objectives should materials and methods aim at? Secondly, what materials and what classroom action will enable learners' skills to develop as intended? We now look at some accounts of the major objectives of oral materials.

8.2 Rivers and Temperley's view

Rivers and Temperley (1978) provide a diagram (see Figure 2) which represents the processes involved in learning to communicate and which distinguishes between skill-using and skill-getting. The authors make two points about the schema. Firstly, skill-getting and skill-using do not represent successive stages in language learning: even beginners have skills they can use to communicate at least something. Secondly, there is a gap to be 'bridged' between the two processes: activities must be designed to help learners to make the transition. For this they suggest using *pseudo-communicative* skill-getting activities, which would lead 'naturally into spontaneous communication' (1978:5).

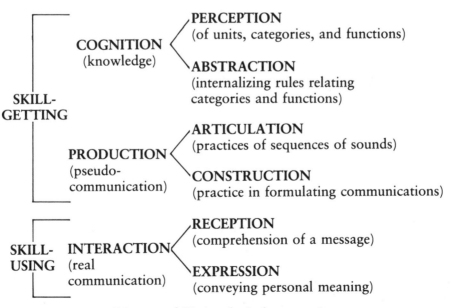

Figure 2: Rivers and Temperley's framework (1978:4)

Clearly, language courses should be mainly concerned with developing skills, that is, skill-getting. The relationship between using and getting skills, however, is for many teachers a central problem of language teaching.

▶ TASK 44

Try applying the terms 'skill-getting' and 'skill-using' to the activities in a unit of a coursebook you are familiar with. Can you say whether skill-getting and skill-using occur:

in different activities?
in the same activities?

Are accuracy skills used in interaction? Where do they appear in the diagram? Should comprehension skills be developed? Where are they found in the figure?

You might like to see if there are any significant differences between Rivers and Temperley's chart and our diagram (Unit 6).

Rivers and Temperley contrast two views of language learning, the *progressive development* view, and the *immediate communication* view. The former holds that 'ability to speak the language derives from the systematic study of grammar, phonology and lexicon': language use can occur only after the learner has learnt the grammar and vocabulary of the language. The *immediate communication* view believes 'that speaking skill is developed from the [earliest] contact with the language'.

▶ TASK 45

Which of the two views (*progressive development* or *immediate communication*) seems to you to be the basis of the following approaches to teaching and learning languages?

Direct method   ESP
Grammar-translation   Notional/Functional
Phrase book   Communicative
Audio-lingual   Your course materials
Situational

What is your view?

Rivers and Temperley distinguish between three kinds of activity:

1 oral practice for the learning of grammar;
2 structured interaction;
3 autonomous interaction.

We will look at these categories in turn.

▶ TASK 46

What parts of Rivers and Temperley's diagram do you expect that the three kinds of activity listed above relate to?

Oral practice for the learning of grammar
Activities under this category are intended to help students 'practise the use of grammatical structures and apply the various facets of grammatical rules in possible sentences' (Rivers and Temperley 1978:110), that is in order to present, exemplify, and practise grammatical rules. Techniques often included blank-filling and various kinds of syntactic manipulation. As we have seen (Unit 2), these can be unsatisfactory as oral exercises, particularly if originally intended as written activities.

Structure-orientated exercises for systematic oral practice (such as pattern drills) can be useful for purposes of demonstration and familiarization:

> [Such exercises] serve an *introductory function*. They are useful only as a preliminary to practice in using the new structural variations in some natural interchange, or for *review and consolidation* of the use of certain structures when students seem in doubt.
> (Rivers and Temperley 1978:120)

In either case, as many teachers would doubtless agree, students should 'understand the changes in meaning they are effecting by the variations they are performing' (1978:120).

▶ TASK 47

What sorts of memory and manipulation problems might you expect when using complex manipulation or blank-filling techniques for oral exercises?

Check a sample of exercises from a course book you are familiar with. Note down any examples of oral activities which might be better suited to written practice.

Would you consider the two uses which Rivers and Temperley advise for pattern drills to be more concerned with: (a) knowledge, or (b) skills?

Structured interaction
Here Rivers and Temperley are concerned with exercises which can bridge the gap between knowledge of the rules and the students' ability to express their own meanings.

> Searle calls language *'rule-governed intentional behaviour'*. We can help the student internalize the rules; we cannot supply the intention, although we can stimulate it by contriving situations and encounters.
> (1978:16)

The authors' point is that it is necessary to lead from knowledge of rules towards communication 'by providing practice in *pseudo-communication*'. This is the 'bridge':

> This is communication in which the content is structured by the learning situation, rather than springing autonomously from the mind and emotions of the student. *We bridge the gap to true communication by encouraging the student to use these structured practices for autonomous purposes from the early stages.*
> (1978:16–17, authors' italics)

▶ ## TASK 48
Which of the following kinds of structures do you think that the authors have in mind for organizing 'pseudo-communicative' practice:

sentence structures
structures of talks
the typical structure of telephone conversations
useful phrases
verb group structures
typical service encounters
useful ways of structuring definitions, examples, and explanations.

Consider briefly some of the terms used by the authors. If you are at work, in the bank, in a restaurant, in a science class, are you in a 'structured' situation or an 'autonomous' situation? Is 'true communication' generally entirely spontaneous?

An example of 'pseudo-communication' is the use of dialogue techniques for presenting new language. This might include 'direct method' techniques in which samples of language are presented as if in a kind of conversation. It is often accompanied by realia, visual aids, or sequences of actions by the teacher or students.

Rivers and Temperley also include dialogues here, as well as oral reports and gapped dialogues. Oral reports may be short (four or five sentences) and, initially at least, take the form of group work. Gapped dialogues involve using recorded dialogues with gaps left for the learner to slot in an appropriate utterance. They propose a checklist for writing, rewriting, or choosing dialogues. The list includes points like:

whether the purpose is grammar-demonstration, conversation-facilitation, or recreational;
the interest and naturalness of the communicative content;
the interest and naturalness of its language;
whether the focus on language items is successful;

the length of the dialogue and of utterances;
inclusion of an element of revision;
possibilities of exploitation.

▶ **TASK 49**

Number the points listed above in order of importance to you. Are there any significant omissions?

> The aim is to reduce the number of decisions concerning the management of interaction (i.e. turn-taking and agenda-management, including message selection), so that learners can concentrate on the development of processing skills, accuracy skills, and gradually improve their ability to negotiate meaning.

How far do you think this represents the aims of bridging activities? How do oral reports and gapped dialogues do this?

How can gapping be graded to control for the learner's involvement in the procedures of negotiating meaning?

Autonomous interaction

Autonomous interaction can be an intimidating challenge, according to Rivers and Temperley. As we have seen, they view autonomous interaction as basically a matter of translating personal meanings into language:

> Students must learn early to express their personal intentions through all kinds of familiar and unfamiliar recombinations of the language elements at their disposal. The more daring they are in linguistic innovation, the more rapidly they progress.
> (1978:46)

▶ **TASK 50**

Consider the implications of this view for learning in general. Would you agree with it in relation to improving one's command of a *first* language in different social and professional circumstances?

In order to help students succeed in autonomous interaction, the authors stress the importance of creating opportunities for students to use the second or foreign language 'for the normal purposes of language in relation to others' (1978:46). There are two points worth emphasizing here. Firstly, the teacher is to be alert and sensitive to the opportunities for interaction which may arise or which may be fostered in the classroom. Secondly, it is necessary for the learners to be engaged in using language for various *purposes*. Rivers and Temperley list fourteen 'categories of language use', such as:

1 Establishing and maintaining social relations
2 Expressing one's reactions
3 Hiding one's intentions
✓4 Talking one's way out of trouble
✓5 Seeking and giving information
✓6 Learning or teaching others to do or make something
7 Conversing over the telephone
8 Solving problems
9 Discussing ideas
10 Playing with language
11 Acting out social roles
12 Entertaining others
13 Displaying one's achievements
14 Sharing leisure activities.
(1978:47)

▶ TASK 51

Do your learners already use their first language for any or all of the purposes listed above? And the second language? You could use a questionnaire, interviews, or class discussion to find out.

Secondly, here are examples of activities which would involve some of the purposes listed above. Can you match the activities to the purposes?

1 greetings, apologies, complaints
2 hobbies
3 reporting on activities, projects
4 crossword puzzles; spelling games
5 looking at an exhibition, TV programme, slides
6 activities associated with festivities, national holidays, or typical customs, etc.
7 questionnaires, surveys, interviews
8 preparing and acting out TV or radio programmes.

Can you think of classroom situations which could be used or created for the remaining uses of language?

It might be useful to compare the 'pseudo-communicative' activities with these autonomous ones.

Are the autonomous ones unstructured?
And in what ways are the language purposes different?

Rivers and Temperley's types of activities cover most of the knowledge which we reviewed earlier. It might be useful, however, to look at one or two more systems of classification of oral interaction tasks.

8.3 Littlewood's view

Littlewood (1981) provides another framework for defining exercises. He suggests that we need four major kinds of language-learning exercise (see Figure 3).

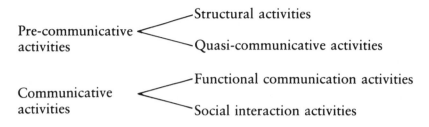

Figure 3 (from Littlewood 1981:86)

Littlewood makes a primary distinction between pre-communicative and communicative activities. The former are preparatory activities, intended to prime learners for the second type of task, in which they are required to communicate.

> In *pre-communicative* activities, the teacher isolates specific elements of knowledge or skill which compose communicative ability, and provides the learners with opportunities to practise them separately. The learners are thus being trained in the part-skills of communication rather than practising the total skill to be acquired. (Littlewood 1981:85)

The aim at this point then is for the learners to practise using acceptable language with reasonable fluency, without being concerned 'to communicate meanings effectively'.

Communicative tasks, on the other hand, require the learner to 'integrate his pre-communicative knowledge and skills' into the full activity of communicating meanings, providing what Littlewood calls 'whole-task practice':

> In considering how people learn to carry out various kinds of skilled performance, it is often useful to distinguish between (a) training in the *part-skills* of which the performance is composed and (b) practice in the *total skill*, sometimes called 'whole-task practice'. [. . .] In foreign language learning our means for providing learners with whole-task practice in the classroom is through various kinds of communicative activity, structured in order to suit the learners' level of ability. (1981:17)

▶ TASK 52

Try applying Littlewood's distinction to driving a car; swimming; or playing a musical instrument.

Littlewood's two major categories are each sub-divided. The first type of pre-communicative activity consists of structural exercises, focusing on the grammatical system and on ways in which linguistic items can be combined.

Littlewood calls the second kind of pre-communicative activity 'quasi-communicative'. This consists of one or more typical conversational exchanges. Some resemble drills, but others are closer to dialogues. Here are one or two examples.

1 **P:** By the way, has John written that letter yet?
  S: Yes, he wrote it yesterday.
  P: Has he seen the film yet?
  S: Yes, he saw it yesterday (etc.).

2 **P:** Shall we go to the cinema?
  S: Oh no, I don't feel like going to the cinema.
  P: Shall we go to the cinema?
  S: No, I'd rather go to the park.

3 **P:** Paris is the capital of Belgium.
  S: No it isn't. It's the capital of France.

4 (working from a plan)
  P: Excuse me, where's the post office?
  S: It's near the cinema.
  P: Excuse me, where is the bank?
  S: It's opposite the theatre.

5 **A:** Shall we go to the cinema?
  B: No, I'd rather go to a concert.
  A: What kind of concert?
  B: I'd like to hear some jazz.
(Littlewood 1981:10–13)

These 'quasi-communicative activities' are intended to help the learner relate forms and structures to three typical kinds of sentence meanings:

1 *Communicative function*: for instance, how to use interrogatives in order to ask questions, to make suggestions, requests, or invitations; how to apologize or complain.

2 *Specific meaning*: for example the use of language to convey real information, real facts, or the students' real opinions.

3 *Social context*: for instance polite conversation, planning outings, exchanging opinions, making and accepting invitations.

▶ TASK 53

Littlewood fits each of these three categories to the preceding examples of dialogues. Which do you think match which?

What view of learning is implied by these activities?

Drills and dialogues can be combined so as to provide a bridge from formal exercises to communicative use. Here are some ways of doing this:

1 A four-line dialogue, with particular substitutions to be chosen by both speakers.
2 A timetable, statistical table, map, consumer's comparison chart or price list (showing holiday or hotel prices, for example). Students' roles are to ask for or give specific information.
3 Situational dialogues allowing repeated use of the same structure: for example, customs baggage check; buying from a list over a shop counter; asking about accommodation in an agency.

▶ TASK 54

You might wish to list any published examples of these and other ways of combining drills and dialogues that you know of.

If these activities provide a transition from drills to interaction practice, then they should involve the learner in more decision making than normal drills. Is this the case? Check by noting down the kinds of decisions involved in two or three typical example activities.

Littlewood's 'communicative' activities, his second major type of activity, are also of two kinds: 'functional communication activities' and 'social interaction activities'.

In the case of functional communication activities,

> the main purpose [. . .] is that learners should use the language they know in order to get meanings across as effectively as possible. Success is measured primarily according to whether they cope with the communicative demands of the immediate situation.
> (1981:20)

In these tasks, 'learners have to overcome an information gap or solve a problem', so that they are working 'towards a definite solution or decision', that is, towards a single right answer (1981:22). By 'information gap', Littlewood means a type of activity in which one or more of the students has to get information from somewhere or someone else.

Social interaction activities, on the other hand, involve exploiting simulation and role-playing.

[These create] a wider variety of social situations and relationships than would otherwise occur. Success is now measured not only in terms of the functional effectiveness of the language, but also *in terms of the [social] acceptability of the forms that are used.* (1981:20–21)

'Social interaction' activities may well consist of exactly the same tasks as 'functional communication' activities, but with an added 'clearly defined social context' (1981:43).

 ## TASK 55

What difference is there between social interaction activities and functional communication activities in the way success is measured?

Here are three hypotheses. Which do you agree with? How could you test your view?

1 Even if success in communicative activities is limited, it is still possible that they help promote greater accuracy and fluency.
2 If success in communicative activities occurs, it is less important than promoting accuracy.
3 It is not possible to assess success in communicative activities.

Suppose someone suggested that you could not invent tasks only for functional communication or only for social interaction. What would your response be? How could you test the claim?

Littlewood suggests that the language used in communicative activities may be controlled by the instructions and information which the teacher provides for the learners. This means controlling the freedom the speaker may have to make 'interaction' decisions.

TASK 56

In Unit 3 we discussed features of normal oral language, and in Unit 4 we discussed interaction decisions. How do these fit into Littlewood's scheme?

It is possible that the sequence of the four activity types is intended to correspond to the kind of progression that learners can be expected to follow. An alternative view might be that functional communication and social interaction can begin very early.

How might your school or language department start to investigate how your learners manage?

Littlewood also looks more closely at different subtypes of his two main types of 'communicative' activity. We will discuss his distinctions and definitions in the next unit. First we will look briefly at one further way of categorizing oral activities.

8.4 Interaction criteria

A number of writers—in particular, Long and Porter (1985)—claim that some aspects of the language of learners vary according to how many of the learners have information to be communicated. Where only one of the learners has information to give, the tasks have been called 'one-way' tasks. In such tasks, listeners simply have to understand and perhaps record the information they receive. In 'two-way tasks', all participants have information to give in order to reach a solution.

The principal language differences that have been noted are that 'two-way' tasks generate more talk, and more use of negotiation procedures for precision of meaning.

▶ TASK 57

Why might the interaction be affected by the number of people who have information to give? What difference is it likely to make if both participants have a responsibility for seeing that information is communicated?

Have you any information or experience which might confirm or disconfirm this view? What is your intuitive opinion? How might you get such information?

A related feature of communication tasks has been discussed by Anderson (1985) in terms of the initial distribution of information. Anderson suggests that another variable with a similar effect to those noted by Long and associates is the availability to both speakers of some common 'shared' information, as well as the existence of different information which both speakers may have to contribute.

▶ TASK 58

What features of negotiation of meaning are likely to be brought into play by the fact that both participants in an activity initially have some similar information? You might consider the likely effect on their understanding of the task and of the other speaker on their own communication.

8.5 Conclusion

To conclude this unit, we have seen that methodologists have in the past proposed activities of two main kinds: accuracy activities and communicative activities. Rivers and Temperley suggest a three-way division; Littlewood a binary division. All agree on the need for basic accuracy activities. Rivers and Temperley suggest that pseudo-communicative activities can be graded and structured. Littlewood introduces 'quasi-communicative' activities whose main purpose is to demonstrate to the learner the kinds of contextual meanings that structures can have.

Littlewood divides communicative activities into two main kinds, implying that these have different learning objectives, and presumably that they involve different interaction skills. For him both kinds of communicative activities can be graded. For Rivers and Temperley, on the other hand, communication resembles artistic communication: it is spontaneous and unstructured (and hence presumably ungradable). It is defined in terms of the kinds of communicative problem situations which learners have to be able to cope with.

 ### TASK 59

Which of these systems seems more comprehensive and useful?

Other important aspects of these tasks are whether they are one-way or two-way; and whether they offer 'shared' initial information.

TASK 60

How far do these elements match those outlined in the schema in Unit 6?

Would it be useful to be able to predict language production if you simply saw a description of an activity? Could you?

The purpose of this unit has been to consider the frameworks used by some methodologists to define the kinds of oral activities that have been developed and used in the classroom. In the next unit we look more closely at the sorts of activities which the authors include in each category.

9   Interaction activities

9.1 Introduction

In this unit we look more closely at the kinds of interaction activities which methodologists have proposed. Here the question is not what aims we should have, but rather, what kinds of activities have been employed for attaining them. Activities can be grouped in terms of topic; information routines; interaction routines; or in terms of behavioural criteria (such as whether one person is being asked to draw something, make something, or arrange something). Our main interest is to see how certain aspects of oral ability, particularly interaction skills, can be promoted through the various types of materials that have been identified.

9.2 Interaction activities: Littlewood

Littlewood's first set of activities intended to practise interaction skills are called 'functional communication' activities, and they involve only the communication of information. He presents four main kinds of these activities:

1 Sharing information with restricted co-operation:
   – Identifying one picture from a set: **A** has the set, **B** has just one of the pictures. **A** has to discover which one **B** is holding.
   – Discovering identical pairs: one student has to find which of four others has the same picture as his.
   – Discovering sequences or locations: **A** has a particular sequence of pictures, and **B** has to arrange his in the same sequence.
   – Discovering missing information: two learners each have an incomplete table and each has to get missing information from the other.
   – Discovering missing features: one learner has a picture, and his partner has the same with features missing; the learner with the complete picture has to discover missing information.
   – Discovering secrets: guessing games, like 'Twenty Questions'.

▶   TASK 61

What aspects of oral interaction are relatively 'restricted' in the preceding activities? Select features from the following list and decide whether they are restricted or unrestricted: vocabulary; order of speakers; topic sequence; choice of topic; choice of routine types; need for explicitness.

Can these results be explained, and how might the differences affect the communication of either participant? Which of these activities are one-way tasks, and which two-way tasks?

2 Sharing information with unrestricted co-operation:
   – Communicating patterns and pictures: **A** and **B** both have shapes/pictures, possibly with a reference frame or grid. **A** arranges her shapes/pictures in a pattern. They communicate with each other so that **B** reproduces the same pattern.
   – Communicating models: as with previous activity, using bricks or pieces of Lego.
   – Discovering differences: **A** and **B** have pictures which have several very slight differences.
   – Following directions: **A** and **B** use identical maps, but **A** knows the destination.

▶ TASK 62

In what sense are these activities based on 'unrestricted co-operation' and not on 'restricted co-operation'?

Consider the dimension of sequencing of information: what are the similarities and differences between the four tasks?

3 Sharing and processing information:
   – Reconstructing story sequences: each member of the group has a picture from a story; without seeing other pictures, they reconstruct the story.
   – Pooling information to solve a problem: **A** has some information (train times from X to Y), **B** has compatible information (trains from Y to Z), and together they decide on the solution (for example, the quickest journey from X to Z).

▶ TASK 63

How does the first activity in group 3 differ from the third in group 1 in terms of interaction problems? Littlewood argues that type 3 activities differ from the others because they involve discussion and evaluation. What discussion and evaluation do they probably involve?

4 Processing information:
   Problem-solving tasks, for example placing items in order of importance, fixing itineraries, deciding use of money for presents, creating a story from random picture cues.

▶ TASK 64

What sorts of routines are involved in tasks like these?

With respect to restrictions, order the four groups of tasks in terms of degree of restriction.

Littlewood's second set of activities, the social interaction activities, are presented as being of two kinds:

1 The classroom as a social context:
   Using the foreign language for classroom management.
   Using the foreign language as a teaching medium.
   Conversation or discussion sessions.
   Basing dialogues and role plays on school experience.

▶ TASK 65

Without analysing these variations of interaction in detail, what implications can be drawn from the suggestion that 'social interaction' activities involve functional communication tasks in fuller settings?

2 Simulation and role-playing:
   Role-playing controlled through cued dialogues: precise turn-by-turn cueing on individual role cards.
   Role-playing controlled through cues and information: individual role cards containing specific aims, and prompts of things to say, tables of information.
   Role-playing controlled through situation and goals: background information and individual role cards with aims, leading to 'drama-like' dialogues in single situation.
   Role-playing in the form of debate or discussion: background information, individual role cards leading to debate.
   Large-scale simulation activities: extended role play over several sessions.
   Improvisation: unscripted dramatizations, based on individual role cards, but no aims.

▶ TASK 66

In what sense—if any—can we predict the kinds of interaction skills which are likely to be practised in these activity types?

9.3 Interaction activities: Harmer

Harmer (1983) makes a distinction between 'practice' activities and 'communicative' activities which raises some questions about the differences between types of tasks. Oral practice activities consist of the following:

> oral drills
> information gap activities
> games
> personalization and localization
> oral activities.

We will briefly describe what each of these are, relating them once again to our own framework.

Oral drills
Examples are given for question-and-answer drills. For example, four-phase drills consisting of Q-A-Q-A:

> **A**: Is John English?
> **B**: No he isn't.
> **A**: Where is he from then?
> **B**: He's Australian.

Information-gap activities
Students in pairs each have a card bearing complementary information. Each student asks the other for their missing pieces of information:

> *Store list* **A**   *Store list* **B**
> apples 15 kilos   apples
> bananas   bananas 5 kilos
> pears 10 kilos   pears
> cheese   cheese 3 kilos

> **A**: How many bananas are there?
> **B**: Five kilos (**A** writes five kilos on his list) . . . How much cheese is there?
> **A**: Three kilos . . .

Games
Examples include *Twenty Questions, Quizzes*, and *Ask the Right Question*. In the last game, student **A** draws a card which has a word on it. Student **A** asks a question so that his or her partner answers precisely the word(s) on the card.

Personalization and localization
Students use language they have recently learnt about people and places they know. In this example, they have recently learnt the Present Progressive for the future:

T: What are you doing this weekend, Gunter?
S1: I'm visiting Scotland.
T: Oh, really . . . when are you leaving?
S1: Early on Saturday morning.

Oral activities
Students are given cards, some general prompt, or a questionnaire to ask questions in order to get to know the likes, dislikes, family, and daily habits of class colleagues.

 ## TASK 67

Among these 'practice' activities there are information-gap activities and games, as well as drills. How does this compare with Littlewood's and Rivers and Temperley's methods of grouping the tasks?

In what sense do information-gap activities resemble drills, and in what way(s) are they different? Are there any weaknesses in grouping these activities with personalization/localization activities, or with oral activities?

Harmer includes the following as types of communicative activities:

reaching a consensus
relaying instructions
communication games
problem solving
interpersonal exchange
story construction
simulation and role play.

We will look at these in turn.

Reaching a consensus
Examples of this kind of activity include selecting ten objects for a journey; arguing about moral dilemmas; discussing reading comprehension.

Relaying instructions
One group learns a dance, or builds a model (with Lego, for instance), and then the group's members instruct others, without using the original instructions.

Communication games
– Describe and Draw: one student describes a picture to another who is to draw it.
– Finding Similarities: without looking at each other's pictures, pairs of students try to find as many similarities between the pictures as possible.
– Describe and Arrange: student **A** has six pictures in a certain arrangement, and student **B** has to arrange his or her six the same way.

Problem solving
Groups are given a problem situation, for example, they have to imagine that they have survived a plane crash in a desert; with some tools and limited survival rations, they must decide what to do.

Interpersonal exchange
In pairs or small groups students find out about some aspect of each other's experience, or interests.

Story construction
Each student is given a different picture, and groups are to compose a story together. The pictures may be from different stories or sources.

Simulation and role play
Examples include individual role cards for a travel agent and a customer; for five students arranging to meet for a meal; for two interviewers and four candidates for a job; a policeman and four witnesses of a monster in Loch Ness; and art gallery officials and several members of the public choosing a new picture for the gallery.

▶ ## TASK 68
Consider the similarities and differences between:

1 the activities within any group (e.g. consensus activities);
2 activities from different groups, e.g. the two 'Describe' communication games and the instruction activities;
3 the practice activities and the communicative activities, taken as a whole.

9.4 Interaction activities: Rivers and Temperley

We have already seen (Unit 7.1) that Rivers and Temperley present an inventory of fourteen 'categories of use' which they consider learners need to be able to handle if they are to develop 'autonomous interaction' skills. They also provide a list of sample activities which would lead to the language described by the categories of use. They suggest that teachers can use these categories to ensure that the students are involved in appropriate activities:

> The teacher will *select and graduate activities to propose* from these categories, so that the attitude of seeking to communicate is developed early in an activity which is within the student's growing capacity. An impossible task, which bewilders and discourages students too early in their language learning, is just as inhibiting of ultimate fluency as lack of opportunity to try what they can do with what they know.
> (1978:48, authors' italics)

To be able to make an appropriate selection of activities depends on an understanding of the interaction which they entail. Here are the activities (real or simulated) that the authors suggest for each category of use:

1 Establishing and maintaining social relations: short dialogues based on small situations: answering the door; making a telephone call; giving birthday greetings; interacting at a party; welcoming visitors, customers.

2 Expressing reactions: situations requiring reactions to TV show, photographic/painting exhibition, or slide show.

3 Hiding one's intentions: students given a mission to carry out must not reveal it under any provocation; for example, the group decides on a 'spying' mission, and individual group members are questioned by other groups to find out the mission.

4 Talking one's way out of trouble: students are asked awkward or embarrassing questions which they must answer or avoid without making any revelation.

5 Seeking and giving information: interviews, surveys, questionnaires, small projects, involving class members or outsiders.

6 Learning or teaching how to make or do something: for example, a sport, a hobby, a craft, a dance, a game.

7 Conversing over the telephone: social calls or enquiries about goods, services, or timetables.

8 Problem-solving: guessing games; interrogation games like *Alibis*, *Guilty Party*; logical puzzle-solving; project study.

9 Discussing ideas: arising from readings, stories, films; projects; controversial debating topics; short texts.

10 Playing with language: crossword puzzles; spelling games (*Scrabble*, *Hangman*, etc.); nonsense rhymes; charades; word histories.

11 Acting out social roles: dramatic improvisations, based on simple situations and character descriptions.

12 Entertaining others: through producing a show, or concert, a TV or radio-type programme or show.

13 Displaying one's achievements, after another activity such as a project report.

14 Sharing leisure activities: participation in typical national meals, festivities, celebrations, or pastimes.

▶ TASK 69

Firstly, consider the activity types from the point of view of similarities. Are any types particularly similar in terms of 'category of use'?

Secondly, classify the activities according to whether or not they include: a one-way or two-way structure; shared information; pre-planning of topic and topic-organization; the freedom to negotiate turn-taking.

Thirdly, consider which activities may either involve or link into others on the list.

9.5 Interaction activities: Ur

Penny Ur (1981) offers a variety of types of oral activities, including communication games, but also including a wider variety of group activities. These she classifies into three main types: brainstorming activities, organizing activities, and compound activities.

There are several subtypes under each category. We offer some examples of each in the accompanying list.

Brainstorming activities
— Guessing games: guess the object/ profession/ country; (clues: first sound or letter; a piece of mime; strange picture; a puzzle clue).
— Finding connections: between incongruous prompts (verbal or pictorial); combining elements into story; finding things in common.
— Ideas from a central theme: listing objects with the same qualities; listing different uses of the same object; associations; what will you need; characteristics (e.g. of a good teacher, or a car).
— Implications and interpretations: doodles; pictures; sounds; faces; foreseeing results; explanations for strange situations.

Organizing activities
— Comparisons: odd man out; categorizing.
— Detecting differences: picture differences; alibi.
— Putting in order: picture sequence; sentence sequence.
— Priorities: rating; survival games; features and functions.
— Choosing candidates: grant-winners; heirs; prisoners; victims; teachers.
— Layout problems: animals in a zoo; dinner placings; marital pairings.
— Combining versions: combining two or more similar texts into one which will make sense.

Compound activities
— Composing letters
— Debates
— Publicity campaigns
— Surveys
— Planning projects.

▶ ## TASK 70

How might the *brainstorming* activities be used with a serious thematic topic like one of the following: geography, news, economy, society, culture of the mother country and/or foreign country?

Which of the *organizing* activities involve the following elements:

descriptions
storytelling
logical reasoning
personal preference
comparison.

How could the *compound* activities be presented so as to involve group work; rehearsal (organization and pre-editing); a significant outcome?

If this is a serious classification, then all the 'brainstorming' activities will share some interactional features; so will those classed as 'organizing activities'. The reader may like to consider some of the following questions:

— How is it decided who will speak next in guessing games?
— What implications, if any, do the activities have for the negotiation of topic?
— Are there any restrictions likely on turn-taking or topic selection in an activity of listing ideas from a central theme?
— Do the activities share any 'routine' features?

The purpose here has been to study the way in which authors group activities. It can be noted that many, though not all, of the classification systems take into consideration external factors like topic or dialogue, rather than the kinds of skill which are to be practised. In the next unit we look more closely at the features of specific interaction activities.

10 Activities for oral practice

10.1 Introduction

In this unit, we will look at some of the materials for practising oral skills in the classroom. In some cases, the activities form parts of integrated language courses. In others they have been published separately, as supplementary materials. Clearly, it is not possible to include reference to everything published in this area of teaching. Rather, the aim is to refer to representative samples of materials that are currently available.

Here we are mainly concerned with four types of materials for interaction skills. These are:

1 Information-gap activities
2 Communication games
3 Simulations
4 Project-based activities.

Our main aim is to consider the kinds of oral skills that the materials are likely to practise. In order to assess the materials, we will be referring to the criteria already discussed in earlier units (3, 4, 6, and 8).

10.2 Information-gap activities

One of the earliest publications in this category was *Tandem*, by Matthews and Read. The book is divided into two parts, A and B, each exercise consisting of complementary worksheets A and B (two-way tasks in each case). Students work in pairs, one with each part. The material consists of fictitious graphics and/or charts or tables to be completed. The information to be transmitted is present in pictorial or note form on the speaker's page, and is communicated either when asked for by one's partner, or because the speaker deduces that if he—the speaker—has the information, his partner does not. Activities include instructions (giving directions), descriptions, comparisons, and narrations. The book was published as supplementary material.

▶ TASK 71

Look at the illustrated exercise from *Tandem*. It is called 'Passport descriptions'. Two or three aspects of the materials can help the speakers to cope with the task. Consider the following aspects:

Name		Andrew Martin		John Grant
Age	47			
Job			Housewife	Actor
Country	U.S.A.	England		Ireland

Name	Sue Turner		Linda Williams	
Age		32	25	29
Job	Teacher	Postman		
Country			Scotland	

the predictability of the vocabulary and the information;
the likely effect of this on the communication;
the amount of negotiation needed;
the amount of likely listener reaction;
the amount of preparatory explanation by the speaker.

How much preparation would one of these exercises need, do you think? (It will of course depend on the level.)

How far could an exercise like one of these be followed up?

How closely does this resemble a drill?

What proficiency level is this type of material best used with?

Note: there are more complex and less controlled types of information-gap activities, for instance Geddes and Sturtridge, 1981.

10.3 Communication games

Another similar publication is *Communication Games* by Rixon and Byrne. This is not a book of ready-made activities, but a set of sample activities which teachers can adapt for specific situations. Some are described in terms of the actions which the participants have to perform in order to complete the tasks. For example:

Describe and Draw
Describe and Arrange
Find the Difference
Ask the Right Question.

In 'Describe and Draw' activities, one student describes a picture, and the other(s) draw it. In 'Describe and Arrange', one student describes a structure made of rods, match sticks or simple objects and the other(s) reconstruct it without seeing the original. This can take the form of a sequence of instruction. For 'Find the Difference', two students each have a picture, one slightly different from the other. Without seeing each other's pictures, they must winkle out the differences. 'Ask the Right Question' is an activity in which a student takes a card on which a word is printed. He or she has to elicit just that word from the others by asking as few questions as possible.

A second similar kind of activity is included in the collection which is not, however, presented under a behavioural label. Examples include 'Complete It', and 'What's my Country?' In the first of these activities the students each have a picture from a story sequence (presented as a strip cartoon) and, without seeing each other's pictures, must put together the story orally. 'What's my Country?' is a guessing game, in which a student takes a card which has the name of a country on. The others then have to attempt to discover the country, asking as few questions as possible.

▶ ## TASK 72

Consider the predictability aspect of the tasks. How far is the information content predictable from the information either learner has? How predictable is the language or the questions? How predictable are the procedures followed? How far can the material enter into a wider scheme of work?

Refer to 'Find the Difference'. How far are each of the activities mentioned one-way or two-way tasks? How far are the learners likely to have to negotiate turn-taking, topic selection, and meaning expression?

Now consider the picture story, 'Complete It', (reproduced above from *Progressive Picture Composition* by Donn Byrne, published by Longman). Consider the possible effects of changing the following variables:

1 Changing the number of pictures from 4 to 6, 8, or 10.
2 Changing the number of participants similarly.
3 Not allowing any group members to see one or two of the pictures.
4 Allowing the participants only a limited amount of time to look at their pictures.
5 Making it into a speed-competition.
6 Expecting the groups to retell the story publicly, or write it independently, or in groups.

Which of these conditions might well cause very short turns and more approximations, and which might cause more careful preparation, rehearsal, and cross-checking? Which might encourage the fullest participation of all group members? Which might encourage more one-way interaction, and which more two-way interaction?

Other relevant questions may be asked about the similarities or differences between the activities. Is 'Describe and Draw' different from 'Describe and Arrange'? If so, in what way(s)? And is the instructional element of a map-reading task distinct from the instructional element of the 'Describing' tasks? Clearly there is scope for finer definition of the task in terms of types of resulting conversational behaviour.

▶ TASK 73

Consider the dimension of shared knowledge. What might be the effects of too much shared knowledge, and what of too little?

Similarly, tasks both with and without shared knowledge are likely to be able to stimulate considerable communication. The question is, under what conditions, and what kinds of communication?

Finally, the language to be used is likely to involve various predictable rhetorical routines. What kinds of language are speakers likely to use for the consensus type of problem task; and what kinds of language in logical problem-solving tasks?

Any answers at this stage are predictions. How far they are borne out in what learners actually do is open to question. However, the questions are of interest, if such activities are to be used at all. The same point can be raised with respect to role plays or simulations.

10.4 Simulations

A third important type of oral activity which can be used in the classroom is the simulation. We will use the term here to denote an activity which involves decision-making, in which the participants may act as themselves or in social roles. It is not performed for an audience, and the participants work together within the constraints of the imaginary setting (see Jones 1982 for a good definition).

Simulations do not as a category provide any basis for predicting the kinds of language skills that learners will use: it depends what kind of simulation is being considered. For instance, a simulated committee meeting is likely to produce one kind of interaction, a simulated interview another, and a simulated public meeting a third. Indeed a single simulation often consists of several different kinds of interaction, including the three just mentioned.

It is however possible to make some predictions, once the nature of the simulation is known.

Simulations generally divide into three phases: firstly, a stage for giving the participants necessary information; secondly, the problem-solving discussions; and thirdly, follow-up work. Herbert and Sturtridge (1979) illustrate this in their diagram, shown here in Figure 4.

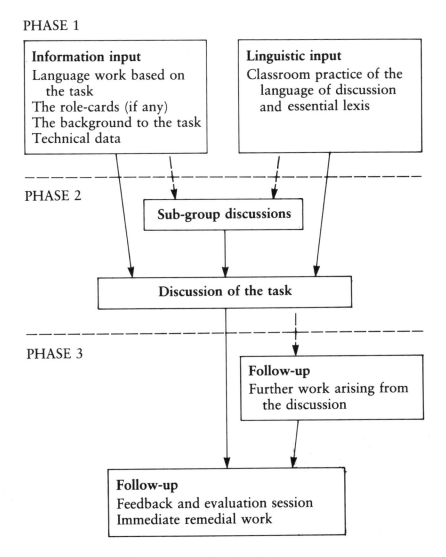

Figure 4: The structure of a simulation

One well-known simulation for language teachers is 'the Canbian Educational Aid Project' (Herbert and Sturtridge 1979), considered appropriate for language teachers in the belief that simulations are more successful if they can draw on the personal experience of the participants. In this simulation, a fictitious country, Canbia, has been offered one million pounds for English language teaching. The question is how to use the money.

First of all, the participants are introduced to the country and given facts about the national and educational background. They read information sheets and listen to recorded tapes to build up a fuller picture. In this example there is a maximum of nine role cards, so groups of up to nine are formed, each with a chairman, and each student with a role card. Students from different groups with the same role card may prepare their positions before the role play starts. The simulation groups then try to resolve the problem, starting from the positions outlined on their role cards. (It is in fact possible for nominal roles to be allocated without cards, for example Minister of Education, teacher trainer, etc., and for individuals to decide for themselves what positions they wish to adopt.) Results may be reported orally or in writing.

▶ TASK 74

Consider the brief description of the 'Canbian' simulation. What interaction features can you predict in terms of negotiation of meaning and interaction management?

Simulations can be more complex and last longer than this one. For example, the group may set up a school (suggested by Ur 1981:115). This could involve financial negotiations; negotiations for buildings; job advertisements and interviews; advertising campaigns; and local problems like parking, catering, or friction between the school and the community. In each case, developments may be introduced through new reading or listening activities, and it is possible for members of more than one class to participate in the same simulation if new participants are needed.

▶ TASK 75

A simulation lasting for more than a single class, running into several classes even, may have some consequences for the oral improvement of the participants. In particular, it may affect their skill at using routines; managing turns and agendas; and in negotiating meaning. How could this be? How could we find out if there is such an effect?

10.5 Project-based interaction activities

Generally, oral work in the classroom will be based on units in the main coursebook. So let us finally look at oral activities in an integrated-skills course for European teenage/young adult learners at the intermediate level: *Challenges* (Abbs *et al.* 1978). We will concentrate on the speaking activities in one unit, entitled 'Something to Say'. (The material is intended 'for students who have been learning English for about four years'.)

The unit in question is centred around the production of a community newspaper. The oral activities include the following tasks: structured or framed question-and-answer exchanges based on the topic; preparing and recording a news report; two 'consensus' discussions; preparing and recording a speech; oral interviewing and reporting back to the group; administering a questionnaire; comparative discussion with a friend/ colleague; preparing and acting out a dialogue; a simulation, whose principal oral components are administering a questionnaire, and conducting a public meeting.

1 Having read and studied the differences between five different newspaper reports about a terrorist attack on an airport, students are invited to 'say what you have discovered about the differences' using the frame: *the first report says that . . . but the second report says that . . .*

2 'In groups think up a story about a robbery, or decide on a current news story that you would like to report. First make a flow chart showing the sequence of events. Then write a group report of the event. One member of the group should record the report which can be played back to the whole class together with the other group reports.'

3 'Listen to what local people think about the idea of a community newspaper. Note down the reporter's questions. Now interview other people in your group about what *they* think of the community paper. [. . .] Report back to the whole group.'

4 Groupwork: Discussion. 'Look at this picture and say what you think is happening. Use expressions like these: [. . .]'

5 Groupwork: Discussion. 'Look at these slogans, and decide what they are about.'

6 Preparing a Speech. 'A new school is badly needed in your area [. . .] Prepare a speech on the subject. There are two ways of doing this. Either you can write the speech out, or you can just prepare notes for speaking freely. Tell your audience what the problem is, who you think is to blame, and what you think should be done about it. Record your speech and play it to the whole class.'

7 Reading and Discussion. 'If you want to start a campaign it is helpful to know what other people think about the problem. You can find out by writing a questionnaire and asking people to fill it in.'

8 Students are invited to consider their circle of social contacts and evaluate what they speak about to each of them. 'Now compare your contacts and conversations with other people's.'

9 Role play. 'Take one of the intentions from [an earlier activity]. Take one of the utterances which matches this intention [. . .] Make it the *first* or *last* line of a little scene. Rehearse your scene and act it out.'

10 Project 2. Simulation Game. 'Take a local problem. [. . .] Plan a campaign about your problem. Write a questionnaire and interview people. Write a report on the results. Do some research on the problem and write it up. Write up the story for your local news broadcast[. . .] for your local paper[. . .] Make banners. Prepare speeches.[. . .] Simulate a meeting to inform the public about the problem.'
(Abbs *et al.* 1978:66–82)

▶ # TASK 76

How do these activities vary on our principal criteria? Which involve the following: rehearsing; long turns; two-way communication; problem-solving; shared knowledge; management skills and negotiation skills?

Do you think that some of the activities could usefully have a greater element of one feature, and less of another? With what effect?

Finally, is there any connection between this project-based approach and simulations?

It is worth noting the large variety of activity types which this single unit contains. This is the principle of a project-based approach, which, it could be argued, is seriously underused in foreign-language education.

In this unit we have discussed in some detail four kinds of oral interaction activity. It is clear that we are still some way from understanding how various activities can help oral interaction skills. However, by observing our learners working with different activity-types like the ones we have been discussing here, we can reasonably expect to form a clearer understanding of what different oral activities can help learners to achieve. This is the subject of the next unit.

11 Students' production in interaction activities

As we have seen, besides examining and evaluating materials on the basis of theories and insights into the nature of interaction ability, it is also essential to find out whether the materials do what they are intended to do in helping the development of particular language skills. If feedback is essential in any attempt to improve what we do, then we must take note of the feedback that we can obtain from our learners.

▶ TASK 77

Feedback is 'information about the results of an activity'. It is used to check on the results, and if necessary improve on them, by comparing the results with the intentions. So for example, the calculations used to decide whether a metal will be strong enough to be used in building construction need to be tested in an experiment. What do you know about the way your students communicate in normal oral interaction outside the classroom? What help do you think they could use? How do you know whether you are right about this?

In this unit, we are going to look briefly at some transcripts of learners working on a communication game, one of the sets of materials for oral production discussed in Unit 10. Our aim is to identify aspects of oral ability discussed in Units 3 to 6. In order to distinguish patterns it is important to be looking for differences between one set of results and another, since otherwise patterns cannot be described. Indeed, we will see that each of the different kinds of skill or ability involves comparison between different sets of evidence:

1 Processing skills can be recognized on the basis of a comparison of the production of different speakers working on a similar task.

2 Skill in negotiating meaning, including communication strategies, can be seen in comparisons of individual speakers one with another.

3 Negotiation of meaning can also be a function of the mutual interaction between the speakers.

4 Management of interaction looked at from the position of the individual can be a matter of personal skills.

5 Management of interaction looked at as a pattern resulting from the interaction can be seen as resembling more closely an interaction routine as a property of the task.

In the activity in question, learners, in small groups of three or four, are looking for the differences between two pictures. In order to compare like with like, we shall look at the way some of the groups start the activity. (Transcripts are taken from Bygate (unpub.).)

▶ **TASK 78**

Is the activity described in the previous paragraph a one-way task, or a two-way task? What sort of ideational and interactional routines would you expect such an activity to produce?

Conventions used in the transcriptions are as follows: pauses are indicated by /–/ for a whole second; /./ for less than a second. The lengthening of a vowel, semi-vowel, or nasal consonant is represented by doubling or trebling it thus: /a biiig mannn/. Unintelligible speech is indicated by / /.

Group A

S1: OK – in this picture in picture – er number one I can see er a little girl – who probably – is inside – her house – er who is playing – with a bear – this bear – it has a brown colour – and – the little girl is sitting – in the – in the stairs of her house – – – – this house is very nice – it has rugs – it has . brown rugs – – mm – – it has – – – – waste basket – it has a basket – who probably serves by er for buying some thing in the market – what can you tell me about the other picture – – R

S2: (with different picture) oh yes in this picture I can see a man erm they'd only . / / er there is a man running away of the room – OK er – in the room there is also a window the window is open I can see through – through it – a man probably – drinking a cup of coffee or a cup of tea something like that – and then I can see . out of the room – a little child that it's by the window – and then there are two pictures – er – – close to the window – and there is also a woman – that it is a stand – and is looking at the man . that is running away – out of the room – that's all

S1: what about you G

S3: (who has two pictures) well I see on my picture a / / of a young girl sitting on a table – – eh – . she's calling on the telephone and – – there are – there are – a – picture flowers I think she's / / mer / / and the other picture I see – – erm – a room where the man is running out – and – – – and through the window I can see a man who is drinking coffee or tea – I er children – – no no I change – a child who is er looking at theee . door – and there are – eh two pictures on the wall – with figures – and – – – and on the floor next to it pictures that have a black erm umbrella and there is a man a woman – an old woman – eh who is eh looking at the – – er – the man – who is running away – – mm that's all

▶ ## TASK 79

There are various indications here that the speakers' basic processing skills are not very efficient. For instance, they are having difficulty in finding the words to say what they intend, or in finding and producing more than a very limited number of words at a time. What evidence is there to suggest this?

There is also evidence in this short transcript that in order to put the necessary words together, the speakers are using some simple compensation and facilitation features. What features does each speaker seem to be using? Is there any evidence that the speakers are using a few phrases repeatedly in the interests of facilitation?

Group E

S1: Do I start   Oh well
S2:   Yes/   / we have two pictures

S1: this picture and this picture . I think I have er / / in an airport or a place like that – erm – there are – – – oh six people . seven maybe . one is running out . theee one of the rooms with aa handbag . another one is – erm – drinking . coffee I think

S2: m right   yeah he he's taking a cup to his mouth
S1:   probably   and therrre   is a lady there is a lady I suppose passing by or observing . and a little boy and er what I suppose is – a kind of . window

S2: yeah

S1: in the corridor aand – ah no . thr'a six people but two of them are part of a – picture I think on the wall so
S2:   mhm   m

S1: I have just – two three men a child and a lady an old
    lady   mhm
S2:   OK – erm – a at the back   I mean er . in the

S2: office I also see a – this is a young lady sitting in a
S1:   mhm

S2: chair she might be a secretary – OK . it seems to me
S1:   mhm   mhm

S2: oh th this er little boy   this little boy seems to be
S1:   mhm

S2: punished don't you see
S1:   mm   yes that's the same thing I have

S2: he has er . he has his . his hands – in the back and
S1:   mm
    looking down

S2: his he his hair his head is down so it seems that he is punished – . this man wh who might be this man

S1: the one – in the window or the one

S2: the theee man er the man leaving the er leaving the office in a hurry

S1: well that man I think he is a robber – a thief

S2:   he might be

S1: because he is running with a handbag

S2: yeah – but that may be er a customer . who is in a hurry he is about to –
he is about to lose her er – – his airplane

S1: well it might be – because his his er . gesture his face is is

S2:   aha

S1: – something special   you feel he is er in a stress

S2:   yes
mhm – that's right

S1:   so the difference

▶ ## TASK 80

The speakers here use communication strategies at various points in
order to express meaning, or increase clarification. What examples
can you find of this? What interaction skill is this: is it related to
explicitness, or is it part of the procedural skill of making sure that
the other speaker has understood? Can these two skills be clearly
separated?

At the end of this section of the transcription, S1 raises the question
of what differences there are. What differences have they found so
far? What have they done so far? How does this compare with what
group A were doing? Have they got any further at this point than
group A at the end of the previous transcription? What do you think
each group goes on to do next?

Consider what processing strategies the speakers use in group E. Are
there any differences from those used by group A?

Are there any apparent differences in the management skills of
groups E and A?

Group D

S3: I have a picture of a girl speaking by the telephone – she is listening
tooo another person that is talking to her in the telephone – she is
sitting down and she's near errrr the stairs – there's a little doll on the
stairs and there are flowers on the table where the girl is sitting.

S4: I have a picture with a girl with a s which is sitting upstairs er hoding
aaa bear/iel/ a bear er a puppy or bear and er – in front of her there is
errrr – – some kind of – er – – erm – chair – and er – the – she is sitting .
in theee stairs

S3: OK and now we can think thre . three differences
S4:   three differences
S3: no?   in mine she's sitting on a table
S4:   right
S4: in mine she's sitting in the stairs
S3: in mine there's a rug in front of her and in yours there's a
S4: er kind of aaa chair
S3: in mine . you can see some flowers
S4: right . in mine – about – er on the wall . you can see a clock
S3: OK so there are three differences

▶ ## TASK 81

This extract falls into two distinct parts. What is the most obvious difference in turn type between the two parts?

What processing strategies do the speakers use in the first part? Consider the processing strategies involved in the second part.

Which part shows more pausing and hesitating, and more communication strategies? Consider the role of repetition in both parts of the interaction. What sorts of co-operative production strategy do the speakers use in the second half?

What does each speaker seem to have most difficulty in expressing?

What do the speakers attempt to do in the first part? And what in the second part? Could S4 and S3 have managed the comparison more quickly?

Which speaker, in this short extract, seems to be running the agenda? What evidence is there for your view?

Which of the two speakers seems more concerned to negotiate exact meaning? Why do you think this might be?

Group C
S1: an old woman is waiting for someone – in the street – no? . that's OK?
S2: yes OK
S1:   ya – – erm – a boy a boy is erm – – – is// is erm – is at the wall
    – – – near to the – to the – – next to the cafeteria
S2:   right
S1: yeah – in the cafeteria is a man drinking coffee
S2:   right
S1: ya mhm – – mm mm – – – er a man is getting . out of the cafeteria er
    with er bags
S2:   right

S1: mhm – merm – – I see here there's a woman who is in the cafeteria – –
S2: I don't have it
S1: no – oh well – – there are some er advertisements of picture behind the
    woman
S2:   right – what do they say
S1: myeah one says mo mo motorail and the other interci
S2:   – above that
S1: myeah you have way way out toilet and buffet
S2: y howbout theee – clock . on the wall – what time is it
S1: the time it's at twelve o'clock
S2: I got ten o'cock
S1: you have ten?/   /
S2: then we have two differences
S1: two differences
S2: yes   how about theee bag – – on the floor
S1:   erm how

▶ ## TASK 82

What production strategies does S1 use in this extract? Consider
turn length, and the facilitation devices used. How does S1 organize
most of her utterances?

What negotiation strategies does S1 use when in difficulty?

Negotiation of meaning occurs several times on the part of both
speakers. Is this negotiation a matter of explicitness or precision?
Why do you think that in this activity it is one rather than the other?
To what extent is the negotiation procedural?

How is the turn-taking managed? Who seems to be taking the
initiative in this and in what way?

Consider agenda management: who appears to be deciding what to
talk about next? How are the responsibilities being allocated for the
task (i.e. what kinds of turns are the two speakers producing)?

How far has this group got in comparison with the other groups?

Group F
S1: I have a pi (laughs) I have a picture of a house it is the entrance of a
    house with the staircase – the walls are painted green and there're . a
    couple of rectangular persian rugs on the floor now at the entrance
    there is a high small table – 'ner on top of it there is a turdlef a black
    telephone and . aaa base containing some green leafs now in theee
    central part of the table there is a . cardholder full of envelopes in the

wall there is erm rou a square mirror . surrounded with wood . and a . a picture a round picture . now in the first step there is aaa five year old girl sitting down . with aaa small brown teddy bear . she seems to be talking and playing with it – there is also close to the staircase a wheel basket carrying maybe an umbrella

S2: all right . in my I have some differences in between yours and my mine picture there instead of a five year old girl there is erm I think maybe a fifteen years old girl she's using a telephone but it's brown – the'rm – there's not a small – t' erm a high table there is a very l low one with some flowers and a vase – with the flowers – a lamp a magazine – there is no basket there is a teddy bear instead of it and there is only one white rug . on the floor

▶ ## TASK 83

Firstly, compare the ways in which the task is managed by this group and by group C. What purposes do the speakers adopt in the two groups? Which of these two involves one speaker describing and the other signalling the differences? Which of these two groups solves the problem by checking the differences point by point? Which uses a single description and leaves the other student to pick out the differences? Which of these two approaches involves a more difficult task of production and comprehension?

Now consider groups A, D, and E. Which approach does each group adopt: one resembling that of group F or group C? You may feel that there is a sense in which groups A, D, and E adopt a third approach, breaking the task down into at least two parts. What is your feeling about this?

In group F, what turn-taking or topic-management decisions are negotiated? Why does this happen? What might be needed in order to oblige these two students to negotiate topic and turn?

There is evidence that negotiation of meaning takes place. What evidence is there? What kind of negotiation of meaning occurs for group F? Why is it of this kind and no other?

What processing strategies do the two speakers use? Are they facilitation or compensation strategies? Are there certain compensation strategies that **S1** might have to use if speaking with a less proficient interlocutor?

Looking across the different speakers, are there any signs, within the limitations of the extracts, of individual formulas? Can you think of any types of language, routines, or skills which this activity seems not to be stimulating?

In this unit we have looked at just a few samples of the oral interaction in just one activity. There are indications, however, that within these limitations, speakers use a restricted number of options in managing the task, and find themselves using a limited number of ways of negotiating meaning, and a limited number of routines. At the same time, there are also signs that the speakers themselves use quite a variety of production strategies. It is information of this kind which can perhaps help us to use interaction activities with care, and to relate such tasks to other aspects of our teaching.

12 Interaction skills in oral language methodology

12.1 Introduction

In this final unit of Section Two, we will look at the way methodologists have been considering the relation between accuracy skills and interaction skills in recent years. First we discuss the general importance of accuracy and interaction skills in the curriculum. Then we consider some suggestions of how to integrate the two. Finally, we look at some suggestions for the use of group work.

12.2 Accuracy and interaction in the curriculum

First there is a contrast to make between two approaches to the teaching of oral language. We will borrow a distinction made by Barnes (1976) between 'exploratory' learning and 'final draft' learning. Final draft learning is learning which concentrates on avoiding error and on producing a perfect performance from the beginning. Exploratory learning, on the other hand, expects learners to experiment with the elements being learnt in order to try out those parts of the discipline which appear to be most useful or interesting to the learner.

Because of the aim of avoiding error, the 'final draft' approach to learning tends to expect various other things to happen as well. For instance, it tends to expect learners to understand things quickly before they come to use the concepts involved. It also expects learners to be nimble and efficient so that they execute rapidly and neatly whatever they are required to do. It expects learners to anticipate difficulties before they reach them, so that they do not have to go back and start again. It expects learners to master all the variables involved for a particular task simultaneously.

'Exploratory' learning also has other predictions, apart from allowing the learner to experiment. Many of them are the reverse of the expectations of 'final draft' learning. For instance, learners would be expected not to understand every aspect of a topic equally well, or remember it equally well, or be able to handle it equally well. It also would not expect learners to be able to plan out a task using the tools of a discipline without sometimes getting things wrong.

In addition the 'exploratory learning' approach tends to assume that personal interpretation can be important in helping understanding, and in improving memory. Incidentally, the exploratory approach tends to expect that a final draft form should become important to the learner if he or she becomes at all committed to using the skills and knowledge of a discipline. The learner's own ambition or self-interest should be enough to see to that.

▶ TASK 84

The reader can probably see that many of the ideas classed under 'exploratory' learning are similar to several of the points made earlier about the nature of spoken interaction. In what ways is the learning of interaction skills an 'exploratory' learning task?

12.3 Integrating accuracy and interaction skills

Earlier discussion in this section raised the problem of what components are needed in a sound foreign-language curriculum. In this discussion, it is not necessary to define 'the learner': all learners seem to be concerned. But how is this principled approach to be realized with different learners? For instance, what if 'the learner' is a beginner, an elementary student, an intermediate student, or an advanced learner? Generally, methodologists have not been able to discuss the question at this level of precision. Nevertheless, some suggestions have been made which may help in the discussion of how accuracy and interaction skills can be integrated.

Brumfit (1979) contrasts two ways of organizing the stages of language learning in the classroom. These are shown in Figure 5.

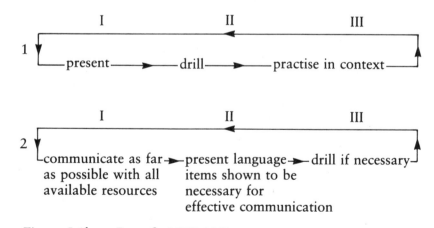

Figure 5 (from Brumfit 1979:183)

In the first case, it is considered normal to start by presenting language to the learners, and then after a period of drills and exercises, giving them some practice. Often the practice takes the form of further exercises. (See Scott 1981:70–73 for another presentation of this approach.)

In the second system, Brumfit suggests the possibility of letting learners communicate as far as they can in the classroom about topics of interest, the teacher only teaching new items when it is obvious that the learners need them. In the first pattern, there is a pre-established order of things to learn. In the second model, what is taught is defined by the learners' needs.

There are clear problems with either approach. In the first case, learners are not likely to practise normal conversation skills; they will not be deciding what they say or how they say it; and the main satisfaction they can aim for is that of reproducing a bit of language more precisely either than their classmates, or than they themselves did on a previous performance. In addition they are unlikely to get much practice, since it will be essential for the teacher to monitor everything they say in order to be able to evaluate their performance reliably.

 ▶ **TASK 85**

> In the second case there can still be difficulties. What problems may arise from the fact that the teacher cannot hear what the learners say, and from the effect that this could have on motivation?

In the second approach, there can be a problem of accountability: work is expected with no obvious reward, either in terms of marks, or praise, or constructive criticism, or in terms of progress which the learner could be made aware of with the teacher's help.

One solution to this problem has been suggested by Willis and Willis (1985). They describe an alternative sequence of phases:

3   Practise ⟶ Rehearse ⟶ Perform.

In this set-up, first the learners practise the new language, either in class or in groups. Part of this phase may consist of observing instances of the new piece of language in texts or in the context of taped conversation. Next, the learners proceed to work on a task in groups. During this stage, learners are rehearsing the language needed, while preparing the topic. Finally, the third phase consists of the learners presenting their results to the rest of the class.

▶ **TASK 86**

> In this approach Willis and Willis have built in two different kinds of classroom organization: what are they? They have also included an element of accountability. What is it? What has been omitted from the previous diagram?

One element that appears to be missing is the basis for deciding what topic to work on next. It will be remembered that Brumfit's scheme specifically allowed the course to be directed according to the needs of the learners. Brumfit's model could still be maintained as a frame for Willis's procedure.

► TASK 87

Try to draw a diagram which would incorporate both Brumfit's student-centred design, and Willis's use of group work and full classwork.

It could be suggested that these three models each correspond to one of the stages of language learning: beginner; intermediate; advanced. Which might correspond to which? Or could it be that all three models could be used at all three levels?

12.4 Classroom organization and oral skills

Practice in interaction skills requires the participants to negotiate meaning and manage the interaction jointly. This by definition implies certain kinds of activities (discussed earlier in Units 9 and 10). There is a connection between the degree of freedom to negotiate and the number of people involved.

► TASK 88

In William Golding's novel *Lord of the Flies*, when the marooned children try to hold plenary meetings on the beach, they discover that they have to have a rule to make sure that everybody does not talk at once. The rule is that no one is allowed to speak unless he or she is holding a symbolic shell. How is this issue usually decided when the teacher is speaking with the whole class? How can this affect the interaction skills that learners learn?

There are various ways of grouping learners in the classroom. Studying the differences between what they call 'teacher-fronted' interaction and 'small-group' interaction in foreign-language classes, Long and Porter (1985) report that small-group interaction allows more talk for each of the students, and a greater variety of talk. Learners spend more time negotiating and checking on meanings in small groups, and they do not appear to correct each other more or less than the teacher does in teacher-fronted situations. In addition, they find that mistakes are no more frequent in small-group work than in teacher-fronted interaction. In the studies that are reported, the activities used were the same in both the teacher-fronted and small-group situations.

▶ TASK 89

Which conclusion do you think is justified on the basis of these studies?

1 That teacher-fronted activities are no better than small-group work?
2 That group work is usually no better than teacher-fronted interaction?
3 That there is a positive reason for choosing either form of interaction on different occasions?

If you can, it helps if you justify your response.

Brumfit (1984) provides the following summary of the argument:

> Small groups provide greater intensity of involvement, so that the quality of language practice is increased, and the opportunities for feedback and monitoring also, given adequate guidance and preparation by the teacher. The setting is more natural than that of the full class, for the size of the group resembles that of normal conversational groupings. Because of this, the stress which accompanies 'public' performance in the classroom should be reduced. Experience also suggests that placing students in small groups assists individualisation, for each group, being limited by its own capacities, determines its own appropriate level of working more precisely than a class working in lock-step with its larger numbers.
> (Brumfit 1984:77)

▶ TASK 90

How many separate arguments does Brumfit present here? List them in order of strength, putting the strongest at the top, and the weakest at the bottom. What evidence do you have to support your opinion? Is this evidence statistical, common knowledge, personal experience, or logic? Would you like to have any more evidence? What evidence would you need to *disprove* Brumfit's point? Finally, which arguments do you think are most important?

There are many possible sizes of groups. Here are a few of those that have been mentioned in the literature: dyads (pairs); triads; groups of four; groups of six; groups of ten; half the class; any of the preceding performing before the rest of the class; the whole class without the teacher. (For further discussion of this, see the volumes by Malamah-Thomas and Wright in this series.)

▶ TASK 91

Here are a few tasks which can be used in first-language education and which can involve different kinds of groupings. Which groupings might be appropriate for which activity?

1 going out to measure the playground;
2 preparing a wall chart;
3 doing a survey of the class;
4 checking or editing each other's written report;
5 rehearsing a sketch or dialogue;
6 preparing a newspaper;
7 having a class election;
8 running a library or materials collection;
9 presenting a talk;
10 having a debate;
11 recording and reporting an interview with a person of interest;
12 preparing and presenting a 'documentary' recording.

Consider the kinds of EFL activities that might be appropriate for each of the types of grouping that we have listed.

It may also be worth considering what language consequences might ensue from having too many (or too few) learners working on any of these tasks.

We have seen that Brumfit noted the intimidating effect of performing in front of a full class. Brown and Yule make a similar point about the simple instruction to an individual to 'stand up[. . .] and tell the class about "what he did at the weekend"'. The authors comment:

> Unless he has been provided with very clear models of what is expected from such a task, this is going to be very difficult for the student. He has to extract from his mass of experience over the weekend some chunk, which can have some structure or meaning attributed to it, and in order to give an account of it, he has to imagine how much background knowledge of the circumstances is shared by the teacher and the other members of the class. (1983:35)

▶ TASK 92

What else, besides the audience, are Brown and Yule concerned with? How can awareness of the problems caused by the nature of the audience help us to use such tasks more effectively?

Brown and Yule comment that whereas a task may be feasible for pairs, with a larger audience the same problem can be more difficult. They add:

> If the speaker has to address a group of five or six other students who

also have to complete the task—under these circumstances the student is more likely to experience a 'them' and 'me' reaction, especially if he is floundering somewhat in a foreign language. (1983:35)

▶ **TASK 93**

What do you think is meant by a '*them* and *me*' reaction?
What effect(s) is this likely to have on the speaker?

Brown and Yule suggest that it is perfectly possible for a learner to need to be able to handle all kinds of audiences:

> [The learner] may eventually be required to address more people [. . .] to give an account of an event which he knows his listeners have no previous knowledge of, or one where some of his listeners are extremely knowledgeable on a topic but others are quite ignorant.
> (1983:36)

▶ **TASK 94**

If this is a legitimate aim for some learners, what proportion does it represent of the learners *you* have to work with? And for those learners, where would you place tasks of this kind: as an aim for more advanced students, or as an accessible route for learning?

Is it in fact easier to speak to large groups, audiences, classes and so on, than it is to speak to one or two individuals, assuming that both large groups and individual listeners are equally unknown or familiar to you?

You may like to test this out by a small class activity. Prepare a list of random one-word topics. Tell a class that you are going to give them a topic to speak on for one minute without preparation. Avoid telling them why. Divide the class into groups of four. The talk for the first topic should be addressed to the whole class. Thereafter, give topics sometimes to be addressed to the whole class, and sometimes in the groups. Ensure that, when it is a group activity, all the groups are working simultaneously.

Under which condition did the speakers speak better? Ask them afterwards which they thought was harder: talking to their groups, or to the whole class?

It can of course be useful to combine various groupings for different stages of the same activity. Roberts (1981) remarks that debates can be difficult for speakers, especially if the topic is complex or emotive. He therefore suggests activities with instructions to the students like the following:

Activity One
Make a private choice. Do not discuss it with anyone. Or form groups of four. You must now reach consensus.

Activity Two
1 Read the case study below.
2 Make a private choice on what you think may be the best course of action. Do not discuss it with anyone.
3 Form groups of four or five and try to reach a consensus choice.
4 A spokesman for your group will report to the whole class what you decide and why, and also why you rejected the other possibilities.
(1981:32)

Roberts adds:

> I would recommend allowing time for students to study the task and the information, and come to some preliminary decisions prior to the group forming[. . .] In each of the [. . .] activities the individual is asked to make a personal choice without discussion.
> (1981:33)

▶ **TASK 95**

Why might the initial period of individual reflection play an important part in this procedure? (Consider the relationship between thought and communication.) How many stages does Roberts' procedure consist of? What is the role of the second stage, and why is it desirable? Roberts says: 'Th[e] final stage is guaranteed to produce a discussion at least as lively as a formal debate, in my experience more so.' This claim compares the procedure with formal debate procedures. How can you judge the claim? What evidence do you have, or would you need? Why might it be a valid claim, at least in some circumstances?

What do you think of the suggestion that group work is always a matter of the same type of communication exercise? What role can group work play in larger class-projects, and simulations? A methodologist has been heard to say that speaking skills can develop perfectly well without any important thought-content. What light does the preceding discussion throw on such an assertion?

The use of group work has often been discussed as if it was a simple innovation which once used would solve all our problems. Perhaps it is just a starting point. And perhaps it might be more useful to talk of 'the uses of different types of group work' in the development of oral interaction skills. There is still plenty of scope for exploration in the use of group activities. Some suggestions are outlined in Section Three.

Exploring oral interaction in the classroom

13   Planning a project

13.1 Introduction

In this section, the focus is on explorations which teachers themselves can try out. In this unit, we go through two example tasks to see some of the things that can be done. In the next unit there are further tasks which can be used as a source of ideas for project work, or as small projects for application to your own or colleagues' classrooms. The purpose in either case is to suggest ways of using our own classes in order better to understand what is happening there.

13.2 Collecting data

In most of the activities suggested in the next unit, the classroom is seen as a source of data. Data may take the form of one of the following:

>   tape recordings (TASK 96)
>   questionnaires (TASK 97)
>   interviews (TASK 98).

▶ ## TASK 96

1 In this task, the aim is to get a general idea of the amount of language produced by learners while working on a group activity. How much do the four speakers speak altogether? How much does each speak? And how much of the talk is in the mother tongue and how much in the target language?

2 The activity: Select two pictures in a 'Find the difference' game in which the task is to find three differences between the two virtually identical pictures. Set up a cassette recorder in a quiet corner, ready to record, held by the 'pause' button. Copy the pair of pictures so that you have one pair for each group of four students. Prepare written instructions: two students are to have one picture, two students are to have the other picture. Without looking at the picture of the other two students, the group should talk through the differences orally. Before starting, they should release the pause button. Allow ten minutes for the recording. On finishing, students should press down the pause button again, and return to the main class. Divide the class into groups of four, and send the groups in turns to record. You can reassure the class that they are not going to be marked, and that you are not going to mind if they make mistakes.

Note: Your first recordings can best be seen as exploratory. Try to keep them short, and as clear as possible. Understanding audio-recordings later can be surprisingly difficult, especially with large groups or whole classes. Also you might find that something went wrong for some reason beyond your control.

3 Do not try to transcribe anything. First, before listening, note down what you expect to hear in terms of quantity, distribution, and L1 and L2 talk. Then listen to the first recording straight through. Is there anything surprising in the recording? Note down ideas.

Now a second listening. Note down the numbers of turns, and L1 and L2 utterances per speaker. You might try the following layout:

	Speaker 1	Speaker 2	Speaker 3	Speaker 4
Turns				
L1 utterances				
L2 utterances				

How far were your expectations confirmed? Are the results similar for the other groups?

Now you might like to listen to your recordings more generally. How else could you use these recordings? Would the recording have been more successful if the group were more accustomed to using the tape recorder? Would it help to re-record the same group or the same class activity, or would it be more interesting to record others?

Note: One sample recording is very little. The students might have had an atypical day; they may be an atypical class. You will need to be very cautious about drawing any conclusions until you have heard a lot more recordings. This should not prevent you looking for points of interest. What would you like to find out more about now?

Note: If circumstances prevent you from recording, then you will have to use some form of observation system (see Malamah-Thomas: *Classroom Interaction* in this series for discussion of this). You may also need to arrange with a colleague to watch each other's groups or classes. It will still be worthwhile, but you will need to think more carefully *before the session* about what you are looking for, so that you take the appropriate notes.

▶ # TASK 97

1 Because you wish to find out from your class how they feel about teacher-fronted oral activities, you decide to set ten questions which will reveal their views. Themes might include whether they feel nervous; how they feel about using the foreign language in the classroom; if they would like to be able to speak the language; the effect of teacher correction;

difficulties in answering questions; activities they like and dislike; whether they have ever used the language.

2 Questions: Firstly, questions can easily be misunderstood, so it may be useful to try them out on a colleague. Secondly, try to make sure the answers are easy to analyse: objective questions produce answers which are easiest and quickest to analyse. Responses might include:

> numbers;
> ticks and crosses;
> yes/no answers;
> selecting an answer from a list;
> expressing preferences by circling a number set out beside the question: 1–2–3–4–5–6, where 1 = least; and 6 = most. (A useful tip is to avoid odd numbers which provide an attractive middle figure, e.g. in the set 1–2–3, respondents may be tempted to select 2; in the set 1–2–3–4, respondents have to select 3 (up) or 2 (down).)

If you really want comments in the students' own words, these should be brief so as to ensure accurate interpretation.

Finally, avoid following yes/no questions (for example, 'Do you like exercise C?') with a question to be answered only by those who gave one of the answers: 'If not, why not?' may encourage respondents to answer 'yes' to the previous question.

3 Prepare a master sheet to compute the responses to each question. Calculate the percentage of each type of response to each question. To do this, divide the number of answers by the total number of students and multiply by 100 (answers/total $\times$ 100).

Now what surprises or inconsistencies, if any, are there in your results? Is there anything else you would now like to know? Are there any questions which you could now improve?

▶ ## TASK 98

1 Suppose you wish to find out your students' views about oral drills. First outline five kinds of question you want to ask them. These can relate to: difficulty; enjoyment; usefulness; kinds of drill (individual, choral); oral and written drills.

2 Select five students whom you would like to interview. These should include one low-level, one average, and one good-level student. Also include at least one student whom you find difficult.

3 Interview them individually, in their mother tongue if this is preferable. Record the interview. Do not hurry them, but try to avoid letting it go on too long, or probing them too deeply. You may want to interview them again on another occasion.

4 Re-play the recordings. Do you find more, or less, than you expected? Any surprises?

5 You may now like to interview all five together. Any differences?

Note: The interview technique is used with individual students or small groups. It can also be useful to get students to talk you through as you play back a recording which they made. You can ask for all kinds of clarifications (who was speaking? what was that you said? what did you mean? why did you say that?).

You can also use interviews to find out learners' general feelings and problems and their ways of seeing things (perhaps to complement a questionnaire). Interviews can be more individual than recordings or questionnaires, because they are improvised. However, your attitude is likely to have a big effect on the outcome: try to be helpful and understanding, speaking as little as possible, getting the students to think aloud. Questions should aim to be WH- questions (why? what?). If you feel that learners may find it difficult to speak openly to you (it happens to everyone inside—and outside—classrooms), this is where a colleague or an outsider can be really useful. However, interviews might also be a way for improving relations with learners whom you find difficult.

14 Exploring aspects of oral methodology

14.1 Exploring oral language

▶ **TASK 99**

In Unit 2 we discussed the difference between written and spoken language. Try this out yourself, in your first or second language:

1 Switch the tape-recorder on and talk into it about a film, play or book that you found interesting.
2 Switch the recorder off, and now write down a similar account of the same topic.
3 Now transcribe your recording. Compare the recording from the point of view of processing strategies. What differences do you find?
4 Get a friend to interview you on the same topic.
5 Transcribe the interview. Note the processing strategies, and the interaction strategies. Compare with the monologue you recorded previously, and then with the written account. Once again, note the differences you find.

▶ **TASK 100**

Record from the radio or television firstly an interview and secondly a discussion. Identify the following interaction features:

1 patterns and strategies of turn-taking;
2 agenda management;
3 negotiation of meaning;
4 negotiation procedures.

How do these differ in the two recordings?

Record a radio talk. Do you think the talk was scripted or not? What evidence is there to support your opinion?

14.2 Exploring oral interaction activities

 TASK 101

In comparing teacher-fronted sessions and pair-work or group-work, it has been suggested by Long and Porter (1985) that there are consistent differences in the amount and quality of talk.

1 Preparations: to check this, take an oral activity and allow yourself a fixed time (ten minutes is likely to be sufficient initially) to do the activity with your entire class. Possible activities: an information-gap activity; a communication game; a problem-solving activity.

2 Teacher-fronted session: record your teacher-fronted session.

3 Group sessions: on another occasion with the same class, select exactly the same type of activity, though not the very same one. Divide the class into pairs, or groups of four. Remind them what kind of activity it is, and tell them that you don't mind what they say or how they do the task, as long as they use the target language. Record as many pairs as you can. You might find this difficult if you have several pairs or groups in a single classroom, because of the noise. One way round this is to try to find a small room where the pupils can record themselves. Groups or pairs can go out in turn. (Barnes (1976) did this.) The more small rooms and tape-recorders you have, the more you can do simultaneously.

4 Avoid transcribing the whole recordings at this stage. Try to identify the numbers of learner utterances. To do this, you might prepare a sheet of paper as shown in Figure 6. In which session did pupils produce most talk?

NUMBER OF UTTERANCES

TEACHER-FRONTED

Teacher:

Pupils:

PAIR/GROUP WORK (Pupils only):

Figure 6

Secondly, calculate the number of errors in both modes. Is there a difference in errors per utterance? To check this, divide the number of errors by the total number of utterances.

5 Results: whatever your results, remember that once is not enough: you may have had an unusual performance for many reasons: you were off colour; the pupils were intimidated (Barnes reported that after a few recording sessions his groups became very relaxed, even joking); it was a rainy day; the topic bored them unduly; they are in any case an unusual class. It is therefore important to confirm your results by comparing them with the same group on a different day, working on other tasks; and with different groups. However, it is not possible of course to get all this information in a week. On the contrary, it is better to proceed slowly, so as to avoid errors, and to allow yourself time to analyse the recordings as you proceed. Too much data will take that much longer to analyse.

► TASK 102

1 Decide on appropriate topics on which learners will prepare a short talk, to be presented to the entire class. After each talk, the speakers can be asked questions about their talk. Record the talks. What features of interaction can you find in the talks? Are there any differences in language-processing strategies during the talks and in the discussions? How might these differences be explained?

2 Try the same thing on another occasion, only this time without allowing preparation time. Are there any differences in the language-processing strategies? Are there any differences in the use of negotiation skills? What might these differences be due to?

3 A third variation: this time, what happens if the learners are allowed to rehearse their topics with partners or in small groups? Once again, what differences are there, if any, and how might they be explained?

4 As a final variation, try the same task in a test atmosphere, using one or more than one teacher as audience. Report any differences that may occur.

► TASK 103

1 Pick a dialogue which your learners are familiar with. Ask them to perform the dialogue from memory. Record their performances, and analyse some representative recordings. How do the results compare with production in short talks?

2 Change the topic, but retain the same kind of situation (for instance, a complaint dialogue about a piece of clothing could be replaced by a complaint about a bit of servicing on the car, or an electric machine that does not work). How do speakers perform—firstly without preparation; secondly, after rehearsal in pairs?

▶ TASK 104

Take three different short interaction activities (to start with you might try one activity based on picture description; one based on a story-telling activity; and one based on a guessing game). Record four or five groups working on each. Listen to the recordings, carefully noting down differences in the lengths of turn.

Look for differences in distribution of talk: which activity seems to encourage more even distribution of talk?

Look for differences in the management of interaction. Do certain patterns appear in one activity but not in the other? Might these patterns encourage different skills?

▶ TASK 105

Most kinds of interaction task can be altered in various ways, which may or may not have an effect on the interaction. Try out some of these alterations in order to test out the effects. In particular, do the turn taking, or the negotiation of meaning, or negotiation procedures or topic management vary in any way?

1 Story-telling: is there a difference between using pictures and using sentences as prompts?

Is there a difference if the prompts are taken away from the students before they start to speak, instead of allowing them to work out the story while still holding on to the prompts?

Is there a difference if they are given random pictures or prompts, and allowed to invent their own story?

Is there a difference if they are invited to reconstruct their own version of a familiar folk story?

What are the effects of giving prompts with a considerable amount of detail, with more or fewer than seven stages to the story, and/or with more/fewer than four participants in the story?

2 Descriptions: is there a difference in the interaction that occurs in a task based on geometrical shapes and in one based on recognizable images?

Consider Littlewood's selection of tasks based on description (see Unit 9): what differences in the interaction, if any, do these various activities produce?

Brown and Yule (1983) suggest that one significant dimension in interaction is the amount of important detail which is involved. What difference does it make to the interaction if highly detailed pictures are used as a basis for the descriptions?

3 Instructions: Byrne and Rixon (1979) (see Unit 10) suggest a variety of tasks which they call 'Describe and _____'. First of all, test out whether

learners produce descriptions or instructions. Then, what differences do the various activities produce, if any?

Instructions based on maps: what differences are there if instructions are one-way or two-way? Anderson (1985) found that if in addition to having two-way instructions, both learners have common information, they use more negotiation procedures. Is this the case with your learners?

With commonsense instructions, is there any difference in the negotiation of meaning, the negotiation procedures and the processing strategies if students work from memory to give well-known instructions or directions (for example, how to make a machine work; how to boil an egg; how to go from one place to another)? What differences would you expect? Do these actually occur?

4 Projects and simulations: one of the points made about projects and simulations (Unit 10) was that as they proceed, learners may become more competent in all interaction skills simply because they are better informed about the topic. Can you devise a way of testing whether this is so?

14.3 Exploring oral interaction and learners' level

In the previous section we concentrated on the effects on the learners' performance of varying certain aspects of the tasks. In this section, we are focusing on the effect on the language of learners doing the tasks at different levels or for different periods of time.

▶ TASK 106

Take any one task-type, and within that type choose a particular task. Record learners of different levels of proficiency from one of your classes working on the same task. Is there any difference in performance from the point of view of any of the major interaction skills or processing skills? If so, what can it be attributed to?

▶ TASK 107

Take a single task, perhaps the same one as in the preceding task, and use it with two classes of widely different levels of proficiency. What differences can be noted, if any, in the ways the tasks are done; and in the degree of uniformity with which the tasks are done in the two classes? (How far do high-proficiency students do the task in the same way; and how far does this occur with low-proficiency students?)

Follow up this investigation by looking at one or two classes at intervening levels of proficiency. Do these classes resemble more either of the first two classes? Can you suggest a way in which the students perhaps tend to develop in the manner in which they do this activity, and in the skills that they use in order to do it?

If possible, repeat the same investigation for other tasks. Do some tasks appear more accessible for lower levels of proficiency, and if so, in what way? Why does this happen?

▶ TASK 108

It is possible that experience of interaction, as much as 'level', makes a difference to performance. Record one of your classes at three or four points over an academic year (that is, once every three months, approximately). Can you perceive any development in the learners' production or interaction skills?

Compare the interaction skills of a group of intermediate students with their performances on an orthodox oral test (for example, the Cambridge oral examinations; one of the examination boards' 'O' or 'A' level oral exams; or a representative national oral test). For this, you and a colleague could test each other's classes. Then compare these results with the performance of the same students on a group task. Does the orthodox examination seem to provide the same results? Can you explain any similarities or differences by referring to the demands of the two tasks?

On a particular topic, compare students' oral ability with their written ability. Is there any difference in effectiveness of the learners in the two modes of interaction? Is there any reason why one should be less advanced than the other? Can you explain any anomalies?

14.4 Exploring learners' perceptions of activities

In each of these tasks, we outline possible research into problems that the learners, the teacher, or his or her colleagues perceive with the learners' performances. In each case, it may be important to consider what, if anything, needs to be done as a result of the questionnaires or discussions. It can be useful to remember that although these tasks are intended partly to help avoid problems and increase the success of the activities, a further purpose is to increase the learners'—and the teacher's—awareness of what is involved. This increased awareness can itself contribute to greater success.

▶ TASK 109

You may wish to find out what your students think about the oral interaction activities which you give them to do. Find out the following, through a questionnaire:

What problems do they encounter during the task?
Was it easier/harder than expected?
Does it get easier to do such tasks as they get more experience of them?

What kinds of task do they prefer?

Which is more important, the kind of task or the kind of topic involved?

Do they feel they could benefit from more specific help?

If so, what kinds of help do they think would be useful?

Would they find it useful to hear what other groups do, by listening to recordings?

Would they mind if other groups listened to their recordings?

Does it matter very much whom they work with?

▶ TASK 110

In a questionnaire, students can often forget some of the difficulties they experienced, because the task is more distant from them. Instead of a questionnaire, it can also be productive to talk with the students individually, or in pairs or even in their groups. Try asking them questions like the previous ones, while looking at any visual material that was used in the task. Ask students to go through difficult bits of the task with you, to help you understand their problems, and also so that they can remind themselves of the particular difficulties that they experienced.

▶ TASK 111

Discuss the questionnaires or interviews, particularly recorded interviews, with colleagues. Try to see if you are not neglecting some potentially important factor which your colleague(s) may be able to remind you of.

Try out problematic activities yourself with colleagues. Try to resolve problems or improve tasks by talking them through.

Compare results of questionnaires and interviews with those of other classes. Discuss normal and abnormal results with colleagues. You may or may not decide to take notice of particular results, once other classes have been taken into consideration. You may also wish to compare present results with previous results in order to see whether attitudes are evolving, and if so, in which way.

14.5 Exploring learners' oral language needs

▶ TASK 112

You may wish to examine the oral language needs of speakers of the foreign language in your country. To do this you will need to decide whether you wish to study the kinds of situation, the kinds of formality, the kinds of topics, or the kinds of roles which learners may wish to adopt as speakers of the foreign language. It will then be necessary to decide whose views you wish to consider: that of the schools; the education authorities responsible for the schools; parents; colleagues; employers; and the students them-selves.

Because oral language needs are likely to become important only after the learner has left your institution, it may be worth considering the demands of oral interaction created by the whole language course offered by your institution.

What sorts of interaction in later classes should learners at a given level be prepared for?

Could oral interaction take a more important role in the general running of your foreign-language course from entry to course completion some months or years later?

Can these demands themselves be planned?

▶ TASK 113

Examination requirements can also have a serious influence on your work. Here are some questions that might be worth investigating:

- What limitations do the exams impose?
- Are these limitations seriously incompatible with objectives for develop-ing oral interaction skills?
- How might the exam limitations be circumvented so that students still get the activities which you and your colleagues may feel are desirable?

▶ TASK 114

Finally, part of the success or failure of foreign-language learning can be attributed to the way learners perceive the use of the language. You may therefore wish to explore your learners' perceptions of speaking the foreign language you teach. To do this you could use a questionnaire or an oral interview. Here are some of the things you may want to find out:

- Is speaking the language evaluated positively or negatively? Examine the reasons. Are the opinions in any way related to performance? Or are they connected with previous experiences; with perception of need; with ideological perceptions of the target culture and of its native speakers; with feelings of lack of aptitude; with a perception of the materials; with a negative/positive view of the atmosphere in the class?
- Consider for each kind of objection some possible ways of perceiving oral ability in the target language in a positive light. It may not be necessary, desirable or possible to overcome such objections.
- What positive reasons connected with later potential needs, and with the language-learning process itself, might be relevant here?
- What other points may provide a rationale for developing oral interaction skills?

Glossary

accuracy skills: the skill of producing language accurately.

achievement strategies: ways of communicating an idea when the speaker lacks the normal words or structures.

agenda management: deciding what topic to speak on at what moment, and how to divide topics up.

communication strategies: ways of achieving communication by using language in the most effective way.

compensation strategies: ways of communicating by improvising temporary substitutes when the speaker lacks normal language.

convergence: shared understanding during communication.

co-operative principles: principles relating to the quantity and quality of information that speakers should normally provide to enable economical understanding.

co-ordination: grammatical device for connecting clauses by addition rather than inclusion.

ellipsis: omission of an element which would be necessary for a sentence to be understood out of context.

explicitness: degree to which information is stated rather than assumed.

facilitation: devices for enabling the speaker to be more efficient in his or her production of language.

feedback: information given about the results of someone's actions to the person responsible.

fillers: expressions like 'well', 'er', 'erm', 'you see' used in speech to fill in pauses.

formulaic expression: set phrase or sentence which tends to be produced as a unit which is typical of the speech of an individual or a community.

hypotaxis: a syntactic relationship of subordination in which one structure is included within another.

information gap: an activity in which one student has various bits of information and the other student has to obtain some or all of it.

information routines : conventional ways of structuring information.

interaction: the use of language for maintaining communication between participants.

interaction routines: conventional ways of structuring typical dialogues.

interaction skills: skills of deciding what to say, when to say it, and how to say it clearly.

interlocutor: a person who takes part in an interaction.

motor-perceptive skills: skills of producing and perceiving sounds.

negotiation of meaning: coming to an agreement on specific meanings using conventional language resources.

noun group: a group of words with a noun as head.

paraphrase: the use of several words where conventionally a single word or phrase would normally be used.

parataxis: the stringing together of structures without using subordination.

planning: deciding on topic, message, and when and how to say it.

procedures: ways of transposing meaning into words and checking understanding.

processing conditions: conditions of time under which language is handled.

processing skills: skills of producing language meaningfully under normal time constraints.

production skills: see **processing skills**.

project: a learning activity in which students do an element of research around a topic to produce a report.

reciprocal communication: communication in which both interlocutors are present and have speaking rights.

reduction strategies: ways in which the speaker can maintain communication by adapting or reducing his or her message when lacking the necessary language.

redundancy: using more language than necessary, e.g. in order to fill pauses, or ensure that parts of the message are remembered.

repair: correction by a speaker of his own or an interlocutor's production mistakes.

role play: unscripted (but possibly cued) dialogue in which the students are given roles to enact.

routines: conventional ways of organizing information or interaction.

schemata: stored sets of conventional knowledge.

schematic knowledge: see **schemata**.

shared knowledge: knowledge which the speakers in a conversation each assume to be known by the other(s).

simplification: the avoidance of syntactic complexity.

simulation: an activity in which the main focus is to reproduce a problem situation typical of the real world which participants should resolve through language.

skills: a hierarchy of decisions and automated actions used as an integrated whole, the lower ones depending on higher ones.

subordination: a structure in which a clause is contained with another clause.

topic: the subject of a conversational exchange.

transcript: a written copy of an audio recording.

turn: a piece of spoken language delivered by a single person without interruption by another speaker.

turn-taking: the process of exchanging the role of speaker in a conversation.

Further reading

The books and papers listed in the Bibliography will provide further elaboration of the issues dealt with in Sections One and Two. The following is a brief selection of other books which have a general bearing on these issues. These can also be used as a source of references for wider reading.

A   On spoken language and oral skills

R. M. Coulthard: *An Introduction to Discourse Analysis* (new edition). London: Longman, 1985.
A good clear introduction to the field which focuses largely, but not exclusively, on the use of oral language.

J. C. Richards and R. W. Schmidt (eds.): *Language and Communication.* London: Longman, 1983.
A collection of papers providing a simple introduction to different topics in the field.

C. Færch and G. Kasper (eds.): *Strategies in Interlanguage Communication.* London: Longman, 1983.
A collection of articles which discuss major aspects of the oral language strategies of learners, with plentiful examples.

B   On teaching oral skills

G. Brown and G. Yule: *Teaching the Spoken Language.* Cambridge: Cambridge University Press, 1983.
This is a good introduction to some of the major problems in teaching and testing oral skills.

C. J. Brumfit: *Communicative Methodology in Language Teaching.* Cambridge: Cambridge University Press, 1984.
A stimulating discussion of oral methodology, and of the place of accuracy and fluency activities within a communicative approach.

C   On research in the language classroom

H. W. Seliger and M. H. Long (eds.): *Classroom Oriented Research in Second Language Acquisition.* Rowley, Mass.: Newbury House, 1983.
Probably the best, though not necessarily the most accessible, publication on this topic.

Bibliography

Abbs, B. *et al.* 1978. *Challenges.* London: Longman.

Anderson, A. 1985. 'What Can We Do to Promote Good Listening? An Experimental Search for One Possible Answer.' Paper given at Annual Meeting of the British Association for Applied Linguistics, Edinburgh.

Barnes, D. 1969. 'Language in the secondary classroom' in D. Barnes, J. Britton, H. Rosen: *Language, the Learner, and the School.* Harmondsworth: Penguin.

Barnes, D. 1976. *From Communication to Curriculum.* Harmondsworth: Penguin.

Bialystok, E. 1983. 'Some factors in the selection and implementation of communication strategies' in C. Færch and G. Kasper (eds.): *Strategies in Interlanguage Communication.* London: Longman, 1983.

Brown, G. and **G. Yule.** 1983. *Teaching the Spoken Language.* Cambridge: Cambridge University Press.

Brumfit, C. J. 1979. '"Communicative" language teaching: an educational perspective' in C. J. Brumfit and K. Johnson (eds.): *The Communicative Approach to Language Teaching.* Oxford: Oxford University Press.

Brumfit, C. J. 1984. *Communicative Methodology in Language Teaching.* Cambridge: Cambridge University Press.

Bygate, M. (unpub.) 'Communication games transcripts.' From Ph.D. thesis data, University of London Institute of Education.

Byrne, D. 1967 *Progressive Picture Composition.* London: Longman.

Coulthard, R. M. 1985. *Introduction to Discourse Analysis* (second edition). London: Longman.

Færch, C. and **G. Kasper.** 1983a. 'Plans and strategies in interlanguage communication' in C. Færch and G. Kasper (eds.): *Strategies in Interlanguage Communication.* London: Longman, 1983.

Færch, C. and **G. Kasper.** 1983b. 'On identifying communication strategies in interlanguage production' in C. Færch and G. Kasper (eds.): *Strategies in Interlanguage Communication.* London: Longman, 1983.

Fillmore, C. J. 1979. 'On fluency' in C. J. Fillmore, D. Kempler and W. S-Y. Wang (eds.): *Individual Differences in Language Ability and Language Behaviour.* London: Academic Press.

Geddes, M. and **G. Sturtridge.** 1981. *Reading Links.* London: Heinemann.

Grice, H. P. 1975. 'Logic and conversation' in P. Cole and J. Morgan (eds.): *Syntax and Semantics, Vol. 3. Speech Acts.* New York: Academic Press.

Gumperz, J. J. 1982. *Discourse Strategies.* Cambridge: Cambridge University Press.

Haastrup, K. and **R. Phillipson.** 1983. 'Achievement strategies in learner/native speaker interaction' in C. Færch and G. Kasper (eds.): *Strategies in Interlanguage Communication*. London: Longman, 1983.

Harmer, J. 1983. *The Practice of English Language Teaching*. London: Longman.

Herbert, D. and **G. Sturtridge.** 1979. *Simulations*. London: NFER.

Johnson, K. 1981. 'Introduction' in Johnson and Morrow (eds.) 1981.

Johnson K. and **K. Morrow** (eds.) 1981. *Communication in the Classroom*. London: Longman.

Jones, K. 1982. *Simulations in Language Teaching*. Cambridge: Cambridge University Press.

Littlewood, W. 1981. *Communicative Language Teaching*. Cambridge: Cambridge University Press.

Long, M. H. 1983. 'Linguistic and conversational adjustments to non-native speakers.' *Studies in Second Language Acquisition* 5/2:177–93.

Long, M. H. and **P. A. Porter.** 1985. 'Group work, interlanguage talk and second language acquisition' in *Working Papers* 4/1:103–37. Department of English as a Second Language, University of Hawaii at Manoa.

Longacre, R. E. 1983. *The Grammar of Discourse*. The Plenum Press.

Mackey, W. F. 1965. *Language Teaching Analysis*. London: Longman.

Malamah-Thomas, A. 1987. *Classroom Interaction*. In the series: *Language Teaching: A Scheme for Teacher Education*. Oxford: Oxford University Press.

Matthews, A. and **C. Read.** 1981. *Tandem*. London: Evans.

Morrow, K. 1981. 'Part B—Introduction' in Johnson and Morrow (eds.) 1981.

Paribakht, T. 1985. 'Strategic competence and language proficiency.' *Applied Linguistics* 6/2:132–46.

Pawley, A. and **F. Syder.** 1983. 'Two puzzles for linguistic theory: native-like selection and native-like fluency' in Richards and Schmidt (eds.) 1983.

Pinter, H. 1960. *The Birthday Party*. London: Methuen.

Richards, J. C. and **R. W. Schmidt** (eds.) 1983. *Language and Communication*. London: Longman.

Rivers, W. and **R. S. Temperley.** 1978. *A Practical Guide to the Teaching of English*. New York: Oxford University Press.

Rixon, S. and **D. Byrne.** 1979. *Communication Games*. London: NFER.

Roberts, J. 1981. 'Discussion through decision making.' *Modern English Teacher* 9/2:31–4.

Schank, R. C. and **R. P. Abelson.** 1977. *Scripts, Plans, Goals and Understanding*. Hillsdale, NJ: Erlbaum.

Scollon, R. and **S. B. K. Scollon.** 1983. 'Face in interethnic communication' in Richards and Schmidt (eds.) 1983.

Scott, R. 'Speaking' in Johnson and Morrow (eds.) 1981.

Smith, F. 1978. *Reading*. Cambridge: Cambridge University Press.

Stubbs, M. 1983. *Discourse Analysis*. Oxford: Basil Blackwell.

Tannen, D. 1984. *Conversational Style: Analyzing Talk Among Friends.* Norwood, NJ: Ablex.

Tarone, E. 1983. 'Some thoughts on the notion of communication strategy' in Færch and Kasper (eds.): *Strategies in Interlanguage Communication.* London: Longman, 1983.

Ur, P. 1981. *Discussions that Work.* Cambridge: Cambridge University Press.

White, R. V. 1978. 'Listening comprehension and note-taking.' *Modern English Teacher* 6/1:23–27.

White, R. V. 1979. *Teaching Written English.* London: George Allen and Unwin.

Widdowson, H. G. 1978. *Teaching Language as Communication.* Oxford: Oxford University Press.

Wilkins, D. A. 1974. *Second Language Learning and Teaching.* London: Edward Arnold.

Willis, D. and **J. Willis.** 1985. 'Teaching the Spoken Language: Variable Activities for Variable Language.' Paper given at the Annual Meeting of the British Association for Applied Linguistics, Edinburgh (reprinted in *ELT Journal* 41/1, January 1987).

Wright, A. 1987. *Roles of Teachers and Learners.* In the series: *Language Teaching: A Scheme for Teacher Education.* Oxford: Oxford University Press.

Index

Entries relate to Sections One, Two, and Three of the text, and to the glossary. References to the glossary are indicated by 'g' after the page number.